THE OPERATIONAL ROLE OF THE OSCE
IN SOUTH-EASTERN EUROPE

The Operational Role of the OSCE in South-Eastern Europe

Contributing to regional stability in the Balkans

Edited by
VICTOR-YVES GHEBALI and DANIEL WARNER
with the collaboration of
EMERIC and MARIANNE ROGIER

LONDON AND NEW YORK

First published 2001 by Ashgate Publishing

Reissued 2018 by Routledge
2 Park Square, Milton Park, Abingdon, Oxon OX14 4RN
711 Third Avenue, New York, NY 10017, USA

Routledge is an imprint of the Taylor & Francis Group, an informa business

Copyright © Victor-Yves Ghebali and Daniel Warner 2001

All rights reserved. No part of this book may be reprinted or reproduced or utilised in any form or by any electronic, mechanical, or other means, now known or hereafter invented, including photocopying and recording, or in any information storage or retrieval system, without permission in writing from the publishers.

Notice:
Product or corporate names may be trademarks or registered trademarks, and are used only for identification and explanation without intent to infringe.

Publisher's Note
The publisher has gone to great lengths to ensure the quality of this reprint but points out that some imperfections in the original copies may be apparent.

Disclaimer
The publisher has made every effort to trace copyright holders and welcomes correspondence from those they have been unable to contact.

A Library of Congress record exists under LC control number: 00111837

ISBN 13: 978-1-138-72789-2 (hbk)
ISBN 13: 978-1-138-72787-8 (pbk)
ISBN 13: 978-1-315-19070-9 (ebk)

Contents

Contributors   vii

Foreword
Joseph Deiss   ix

Opening Address
Einar Bull   xi

Introductory Remarks: I
Marianne von Grünigen   xvi

Introductory Remarks: II
Margrit Wästfelt   xix

Part I   The Operational Activities of the OSCE in South-Eastern Europe

1. A Success Story: The United Nations Transitional Authority for Eastern Slavonia
   Willy Hanset   3

2. Croatia: Status Report
   Bernard Poncet   11

3. Bosnia and Herzegovina: Status Report
   Robert L. Barry   20

4. The Operational Role of the OSCE in the Field of Peace-Building: The Case of Bosnia and Herzegovina
   Marianne Ducasse-Rogier   24

5. Albania: Status Report
   Geert-Hinrich Ahrens   30

6. Kosovo: Status Report
   Dan Everts   37

Contents

7 The Former Yugoslav Republic of Macedonia: Status Report
   Carlo Ungaro 41

8 The Operational Role of the OSCE in the Field of Conflict Prevention: An Assessment of the Spillover Monitor Mission to Skopje (Macedonia)
   Emeric Rogier 47

Part II The Development of Regional Stability in South-Eastern Europe

9 The OSCE and the Stability Pact for South-Eastern Europe
   Victor-Yves Ghebali 55

10 The Co-operation between International Organisations in the Management of the Third Yugoslav War
   Eric Remacle 69

11 The 1999 Istanbul Charter for European Security: A Critical Assessment
   Victor-Yves Ghebali 77

12 Concluding Remarks
   Erik Pierre 86

13 Concluding Address
   Louis Michel 91

Part III Appendices

Report to the Chairman-in-Office on the Development of the South-Eastern Europe Regional Dimension of the OSCE
Robert L. Barry 95

Istanbul Summit Declaration, 19 November 1999 101

Charter for European Security, Istanbul, 19 November 1999 113

Stability Pact for South-Eastern Europe, Cologne, 10 June 1999 132

Index 145

Contributors

Geert-Hinrich Ahrens
Ambassador, Head of the OSCE Presence in Albania

Robert L. Barry
Ambassador, Head of the OSCE Mission to Bosnia and Herzegovina, Special Envoy of the Chairman-in-Office of the OSCE 1999

Einar Bull
Ambassador, Representative of the Chairman-in-Office of the OSCE, Norwegian Chairmanship 1999, Norwegian Royal Ministry of Foreign Affairs

Joseph Deiss
Federal Councillor, Federal Department of Foreign Affairs of the Swiss Confederation

Dan Everts
Ambassador, Head of the OSCE Mission to Kosovo

Victor-Yves Ghebali
Professor, The Graduate Institute of International Studies (Geneva)

Willy Hanset
Lieutenant-General, Former Commander of the Military Component of UNTAES, Head of Operational Command Ground Force, Belgian Armed Forces

Louis Michel
Vice Prime Minister and Foreign Affairs Minister, Kingdom of Belgium

Erik Pierre
Ambassador, Former Ambassador of Sweden to Sarajevo, Brussels

Bernard Poncet
Ambassador, Head of the OSCE Mission to Croatia

Eric Remacle
Professor, Université Libre de Bruxelles

Emeric Rogier
PhD student, Graduate Institute of International Studies (Geneva)

Marianne Ducasse-Rogier
PhD student, Graduate Institute of International Studies (Geneva)

Carlo Ungaro
Ambassador, Head of the OSCE Spillover Monitor Mission to Skopje

Marianne von Grünigen
Ambassador, Head of Swiss Delegation to the OSCE

Margrit Wästfelt
First Deputy Head of Mission of Austria to the OSCE

Foreword

Joseph Deiss

The Conference on 'The Operational Role of the OSCE in South-Eastern Europe: Contributing to Regional Stability in the Balkans' addressed one of the most urgent problems in Europe today. During the 1990s, a series of serious conflicts broke out that devastated the region. The commitment of the international community to stabilising South-Eastern Europe is considerable. We are confronted with the challenge of establishing democracy, the rule of law and respect for human rights, in particular the rights of minorities.

The OSCE is making a major contribution to this effort. In the countries of the region, its Missions promote stability by helping government authorities implement and then stick to their obligations. In Brussels, this conference brought OSCE field experience and academic expertise together and facilitated a fruitful exchange of experiences and analyses.

Success in this common endeavour is far from sure. The conference was right to draw our attention to the historical dimension of the issues at stake and to point out how difficult it is to open up established authoritarian power structures to democratic forces. Elections are only an appropriate means in situations where a basic and functioning framework respecting the rule of law has been established.

The situation remains worryingly uncertain in a number of States in the region. The failure of the Belgrade government to lead the country away from the totalitarian structures of the past and towards democracy and solid co-operation with its partners both in and outside the region has undermined the stability of South-Eastern Europe. Respect for minorities – in particular in the context of Kosovo – is one of the keys to peace and security. We must continue to watch events closely and to ensure that the international community gives clear and coherent signals.

The Stability Pact for South-Eastern Europe, which has been placed under the auspices of the OSCE, is the forum for the efficient determination and co-ordination of bilateral and multilateral measures. It focuses international support on pushing through political and economic reforms in the region, in combination with the establishment of reliable structures in the countries concerned. We must follow up a successful start with projects in order to consolidate and build on the transformations that have been started.

We will only achieve our objectives in South-Eastern Europe if the countries concerned, their government authorities and local civil society acquire full ownership of the transformation processes. A paternalistic approach imposed from outside would be out of place. In our efforts, we have to assist the countries of the region to implement the commitments they themselves have entered into. Help should only be given when and for as long as needed, and we should envisage handing over responsibilities to local players right from the start.

I would like to thank the conference organisers most sincerely for their initiative and commitment. This meeting was the successful result of co-operation between several partners. It has been made possible thanks to the material support of the Belgian authorities and that of the Swiss Federal Department of Defence, Civil Protection and Sport as part of its Partnership for Peace programme. Experts from different areas were gathered together, and their deliberations will make an important contribution to meeting the serious challenges facing Europe today.

Opening Address

Einar Bull

The OSCE Istanbul Summit has just been concluded. The underlying purpose of this meeting was to continue the adaptation of the OSCE to new challenges, to emphasise its primary role in European crisis management, and to strengthen co-operation with other security organisations. The decision to establish Rapid Expert Assistance and Co-operation Teams, REACT, will greatly enhance the ability of the OSCE to respond quickly to demands for assistance and to implement large civilian field operations, as will the establishment of an Operations Centre within the OSCE secretariat. With the Istanbul decisions the OSCE is even better placed to contribute to answering the demand for integrated crisis management involving civilian as well as military components.

Knitting the political, military and economic activities of all the instruments of the international community – the UN, the OSCE, the EU and NATO, to name but a few – into a seamless web of mutually reinforcing practical co-operation has become one of the main challenges of post-Cold War conflict prevention and conflict resolution. Work-sharing based on comparative advantages ensures that limited resources are used where they are most effective.

There is broad agreement within the Euro-Atlantic security architecture on the need to address the root causes of instability. Democratisation, respect for human rights and promoting the rule of law must go hand in hand with economic reform. Whenever possible, we should prevent, contain and resolve conflicts before they reach the stage where military force is required. This is the cheapest form of crisis management, in terms of both money and human suffering.

There is, moreover, general agreement among OSCE Participating States that the OSCE should be the organisation of first resort for conflict prevention and crisis management in the OSCE area. This is reflected in the so-called 'OSCE first' principle. At the same time it is of course recognised that the scope and character of the challenges to our common security mean that no single organisation can deal with all the challenges on its own. Hence, the OSCE attaches fundamental importance to further developing its partnership with other international organisations in practical conflict prevention and management by civilian means.

The relationship between the UN and the OSCE is steadily being strengthened. The well-functioning co-operation within the framework of the UN Mission to Kosovo (UNMIK) is a good example of this. The overall authority of the UN is undisputed, but the OSCE Charter for European Security, adopted by the Istanbul Summit, underpins the OSCE's primary role and its position as the UN's most important partner in Europe.

But there is also broad agreement that credible crisis management requires the ability to employ military force whenever necessary, either to enforce compliance or to provide the stability required for civilian efforts to be effective. Organisations like NATO are therefore crucial in our joint approach to European security.

Increased co-operation between the OSCE and the European Union on crisis management by non-military means is a particularly interesting aspect of Euro-Atlantic security architecture that is now evolving. Kosovo is a case in point. Within the framework of UNMIK, the OSCE is responsible for institution-building and democratisation, and the EU for economic reconstruction. This reflects our conviction that without parallel efforts in a number of fields, Kosovo stands no chance of becoming the stable multi-ethnic community we want it to be.

I believe that the role of the international community in Kosovo in many ways represents a model for the future. The security architecture of the twenty-first century will increasingly be characterised by intimate co-operation between a wide range of organisations and regional arrangements based on the comparative advantages of each actor.

What are the comparative advantages of the OSCE within the new Euro-Atlantic security architecture? There are two that are particularly relevant. In the first place, the OSCE is the most inclusive of the regional security organisations. It covers a vast geographical area stretching from Vancouver to Vladivostok. Its broad membership – fifty-four nations, including all the European States, the USA, Canada and Russia – means that it is a useful and politically expedient framework for the co-ordination of conflict management when a number of different international organisations are involved.

The second, and most important, advantage of the OSCE is its emphasis on field operations and its record in conflict prevention and crisis management on the ground. During the past ten years the requirement to prevent, contain and resolve crises and to rebuild war-torn societies has exploded. More and more long-term efforts on the ground in Central and Eastern Europe have been called for.

The OSCE has adapted to the need for long-term presence on the ground. Since the last Summit in Lisbon in 1996, the operational capacity of the organisation has expanded greatly. The OSCE started out in the 1970s as a rolling diplomatic conference, a framework for negotiating and implementing human rights commitments and arms control agreements. This diplomatic conference is now gone, never to return. Today, the OSCE has acquired a pronounced operational character. It has a permanent field presence in eighteen countries or conflict areas, primarily in the Balkans, but also in the Caucasus and other parts of the former Soviet Union, including Central Asia. Their tasks fall under the general headings of conflict prevention, conflict management and post-conflict rehabilitation. The fact of the matter is that the OSCE today is present in some capacity in every potential or actual trouble spot on our continent. That makes it unique among the security institutions in Europe, and adds a special legitimacy to its efforts.

The impact of the OSCE in conflict prevention and conflict management, and its evolving relationship with other international organisations, is most clearly seen in the continuous efforts to resolve the conflicts in and around the Former Yugoslavia. In the Balkans alone, the OSCE has Missions in five different countries, employing more than 3,000 national and international staff.

The operations centring on Kosovo have undoubtedly been most prominent in the public view of the field activities of the OSCE. The issue has indeed dominated the agenda of the Norwegian OSCE Chairmanship to an extent that exceeds what we originally envisaged. Moreover, Kosovo has given us an interesting insight into the possibilities and limitations of the organisation and the need for close interaction between the various actors involved in these processes.

The gradual deployment of the Kosovo Verification Mission before Christmas last year marked an important step ahead in the development of the OSCE. It was a new type of field operation for the organisation, focusing as it did on monitoring and reporting the implementation of an agreement between the two warring parties. As such its tasks were different from the traditional core activities of the OSCE, which include democratisation, establishing the rule of law and ensuring respect for basic human rights.

The KVM operation, however, underscored that we need to be realistic as to the capabilities of the organisation. Kosovo showed once more that the OSCE can only provide assistance in order to resolve conflicts. If the parties avail themselves of this offer, the organisation stands ready to assist in implementing agreements, to help, advise, train and facilitate – to build a durable peace, and to foster tolerance among people who have been involved in conflict. But the main implementation will always be up to the leaders and the people in conflict-ridden areas. The OSCE cannot force the parties to a conflict to accept specific solutions.

Following adoption of Security Council Resolution 1244, the international community has for the first time established a large-scale integrated operation designed to tackle a complex and difficult post-conflict situation. It adds yet another dimension to the operational dimension of both the OSCE and the other organisations participating in UNMIK. The OSCE Mission in Kosovo, as the institution-building pillar of UNMIK, is responsible for crucial tasks like the training of police and civil servants, monitoring of human rights, development of free media and elections. Whereas the KVM was somewhat out of the mainstream of OSCE activities, these tasks in many ways represent a return to the core functions of the OSCE, the building and safeguarding of functioning democracies through the creation of an environment based on confidence and the rule of law.

The organisation and conduct of well-prepared elections in Kosovo will be a major challenge next year. The registration of voters, the preparation of electoral rules and regulations are large and difficult tasks that must be in place before elections can be held. Our experience from conducting elections in Bosnia is invaluable in this context, and makes the OSCE well fitted to carry out this work. The experiences we gain in Kosovo will likewise form foundations for future OSCE field activities.

Our activities in the Balkans, initially in Macedonia, Croatia and Bosnia, and later on in Albania and now Kosovo, have taught us that even when a solution is in place in one particular conflict, it will affect regional stability for a long time to come. Long-term measures to counteract the wider consequences of a conflict are required. We must also realise that many of the problems facing the international community and individual nations are of the same nature throughout the region. This underlines the need to look beyond the narrow confines of national borders, and to build the same kind of interdependence between nations and ethnic groups in South-Eastern Europe that have made armed conflict inconceivable in Western Europe for more than fifty years.

An important area of priority for the Norwegian OSCE Chairmanship is therefore to ensure that both the OSCE and the rest of the international community develop regional measures for South-Eastern Europe. The lessons we draw from this exercise are also proving useful for the OSCE as we develop broadly-based strategies for other areas of conflict, including Central Asia and the Southern Caucasus.

The Stability Pact for South-Eastern Europe is a response to the need for comprehensive, long-term action in this region. The OSCE constitutes the political framework for the Pact, while the EU will be playing a leading role in the implementation. Division of labour between institutions is again the key.

The Stability Pact represents a novel concept and a novel approach. Hence, we should not be surprised that there have been teething problems. But following the inaugural meeting of the Working Tables and the discussion we had in Istanbul based on Special Co-ordinator Hombach's status report, I think we can conclude that the Pact is under way. Several specific follow-up processes have been launched. Now the main challenge will be to initiate and develop concrete measures to make the Pact something more than a framework for consultations.

I would also like to underline that the countries directly affected have a special responsibility for ensuring that this initiative becomes a success. The international community can offer advice and concrete assistance, but we will fail unless we can ensure the commitment of those who should benefit from the Pact.

The OSCE is committed to supporting the Stability Pact. Last July, the Chairman-in-Office tasked Ambassador Barry, Head of the Mission to Bosnia and Herzegovina, to develop in close co-operation with the other Heads of Mission in the region the OSCE's regional dimension. The goal of this work is to improve the organisation's own ability to deal with regional problems, to encourage host country co-operation at a regional level, and to provide support for the Stability Pact. The aim is to achieve these goals in three ways:

- by strengthening co-operation among OSCE Missions in pursuit of clearly defined goals, such as refugee return;
- by initiating regional projects, both to deal with trans-border issues such as organised crime and to use best practices to deal with common problems which are not trans-border in nature, such as judicial reform; and
- by initiating or supporting projects endorsed by the Stability Pact itself, such as the OSCE-supported task force on gender issues and the OSCE proposal for a legislative clearing house and resource centre in the region.

We will focus on areas where the OSCE has specific competence. This may include the development of free media and a civil society, cross-border co-operation, refugee return and ethnic reconciliation, human rights, gender issues and cultural and religious dialogue.

Strengthened regional ties may help alleviate antagonism and distrust between the countries of the region. The approach may also serve to increase the effectiveness of each individual Mission and the efforts of the OSCE as a whole.

By way of conclusion, I think it is fair to say that the experience from operations like Kosovo point to the fact that the OSCE, also in the years to come, will be a linchpin in the Euro-Atlantic security architecture. I believe that its responsibilities can broadly be put in two main categories. Firstly, it will increasingly make use of its status as a regional organisation under Chapter VIII of the UN Charter. As such it will be a partner of the UN, a partner which relieves the UN of some of its responsibility and which ensures the necessary legitimacy of conflict prevention and peace support actions carried out by the international community on our continent.

Secondly, the OSCE will also be a factor in terms of its own expertise. In the areas of conflict prevention and post-conflict rehabilitation, of democratisation, building the rule of law and promoting human rights, it will be the foremost actor in Europe. Also on this score it will serve to relieve the UN of some of its burden.

Introductory Remarks: I

Marianne von Grünigen

The conference of which this volume records the Proceedings took place at the right time and at the right venue. Some of us were just back from the OSCE Summit in Istanbul, where the Balkans, this time in particular Kosovo, had been in the forefront of our political deliberations. Brussels was well chosen as we welcomed the Stability Pact for South-Eastern Europe, the idea of the European Union, which stays under the auspices of the OSCE. If we succeed together to improve the situation in the whole region, we will have indeed brought progress to European stability and security and helped an area that is very close to us and whose citizens also live in our countries, many of them having found a permanent home there.

Since the beginning of the 1990s, we have been preoccupied with the developments in the Balkans, with the wars involving destruction of cities and villages, massacres, displaced persons, refugees in almost all areas. These conflicts have in fact had a great influence on the development of the OSCE, moving it from a negotiating forum to an operational organisation that has now at Istanbul once more been strengthened. The first Missions have been sent to the Balkans. The first big Mission of 200 persons was opened in 1996 in Sarajevo within the framework of the Dayton Agreement. The second big Mission with a similar ceiling of collaborators was sent to Croatia in 1997. In the same year, we also opened an important Mission in Albania. In Kosovo, the OSCE tried one year ago, unfortunately in vain, to prevent the outbreak of an armed conflict by means of the Kosovo Verification Mission (KVM); however, it is now the most active international body in Kosovo within UNMIK, having built up the OSCE's biggest Mission with about 450 collaborators, and still to be enlarged to over 700 members.

One aspect that has bothered us in the past, especially when we had to build up missions of a large size, was the time it needs to elaborate the mandate, and find the right people to take over the responsibilities, before the creation of a vacuum that can be abused by adverse forces. Thus, the Istanbul Charter has now asked the OSCE to set up Rapid Expert Assistance and Co-operation Teams (REACT) that will enable OSCE bodies and institutions to offer experts quickly to Participating States to provide assistance in conflict prevention, crisis management and post-conflict rehabilitation. An operation centre in the OSCE Secretariat will support REACT. The system is planned to be operational by June 2000.

I shall now try to give you a more general picture of the Missions' tasks, and develop some thoughts on the possibilities for a regional approach to the problems in the Balkans. The main tasks of the OSCE Missions in South-Eastern Europe are to be found within the so-called 'human dimension'. They include in particular, elections, democratisation, human rights and media.

National and local elections are of course an excellent instrument to promote the democratisation of a country. In order to obtain free and fair elections, there are nonetheless various preconditions to be fulfilled, such as an election law that permits free and fair elections or some equivalent provisional rules, voters' registration, international assistance in the preparation and performance of elections, as well as supervision or observance. This process has now been well established within the OSCE, with ODIHR and the Parliamentary Assemblies of OSCE as well as the Council of Europe.

Even though elections are part of the democratisation process, democracy-building goes beyond and includes as well the building of a pluralistic civil society, the creation of democratic institutions and an independent judiciary, the introduction of the rule of law by elaborating, where necessary, a new Constitution and relevant legislation such as election laws, property laws and so on. Those activities imply also the training of judges and their clerks and of government officials for the civil administration. Democratisation means also the promotion of inter-ethnic relations, co-operation and tolerance with a view to confidence-building and in the end reconciliation.

To promote respect for human rights means to observe the general human rights situation and report on it. It means also to examine, on a case-by-case basis, individual violations of human rights, to intervene with the competent authorities and to co-operate with relevant local human rights institutions or organisations. In Bosnia and Herzegovina, there exists a local Federation of Ombudsmen, an international Ombudsperson for Human Rights and a Human Rights Chamber. Also active in this field are international NGOs such as Human Rights Watch, Amnesty International or the International Helsinki Committee, all most welcome partners to the OSCE in human rights matters. The most important human rights questions to be dealt with are rights of refugees and displaced persons, property rights, freedom of movement and violation of political rights in the election process.

Of growing importance is the development of free media including the training of journalists, elaboration of rules and standards and respect for freedom of the press. Such media programs have been started in Bosnia and Herzegovina; in Kosovo they are one specific pillar of the OSCE activities.

Besides the human dimension, the Missions deal more and more with policing. This started in Croatia with police monitoring, in particular in the Danube region. It was further developed in Kosovo, where the OSCE has built up a police school, where already the second group of trainees has passed through. After these positive experiences, the OSCE has laid down policing as an operational tool in the

Istanbul Charter and will also examine the possibilities of executing policing in order to contribute to correct law-enforcement.

In all conflicts and post-conflict areas, you find nowadays not only OSCE, but also other international organisations such as the UN, its High Commissioners for Refugees and for Human Rights, the Council of Europe, the European Union, NATO and many international and local NGOs assisting the country to find its way towards stability and peace. In the beginning, there was often competition rather than co-operation among these organisations, which was of course very detrimental to the results of the various well-intended endeavours. Therefore, OSCE has for a couple of years tried to establish a non-hierarchical co-operation with these organisations in the field. Having achieved some good results in the past, the Organisation was encouraged to elaborate, with the active assistance of the EU, a so-called platform for co-operative security that is now an annex to the Istanbul Charter and will in the future help to better co-ordinate the common efforts, facilitated by regular contacts and discussions among the various headquarters. For over two years, this co-operation has worked positively in the field of elections, but it has also increased in other contexts, such as for refugees, for democratic institution-building and for post-conflict rehabilitation.

Another point that I would like to mention and that seems extremely important to me is the following: when the OSCE and other international organisations and NGOs deploy their well-developed activities in a given area, we should at the same time keep in mind that our goal is to assist in creating an environment in which the citizens of the country and all other residents can again live peacefully together and take full responsibility for their public affairs and daily activities. Thus, international endeavours should never become an end in themselves, but always just help building up sustainable stability managed by the people and their authorities themselves. That means we should be able to assist in creating a situation that permits us to one day leave a normally functioning country or area.

I hope to have given you an idea of the OSCE's capabilities and endeavours to contribute to the stability in South-Eastern Europe. As each area in which a mission has been established has its own particularities, each mandate contains also, beside some general elements, some tailor-made activities. However, the longer OSCE is in South-Eastern Europe, the more we are conscious that many problems also have trans-border implications and should be treated within a regional approach. The OSCE started to reflect more seriously about this over a year ago, and the Chairman-in-Office has asked Ambassador Barry, Head of the Mission to Bosnia and Herzegovina, to have a deeper look at this. There is indeed a very important need to develop a regional approach to the area. This has started by more intensive co-operation among the Missions. But it should also help the populations themselves to discover once again how to live peacefully together, including in a cross-border context. The Stability Pact for the Balkans should thus seriously be worked on, promoting co-operation between the OSCE and the EU, as well as among all the willing States.

Introductory Remarks: II

Margrit Wästfelt

South-Eastern Europe will be, of course, a focal point of Austrian activity during its forthcoming OSCE Chairmanship. Austria has a natural interest in the Balkans, as it lies in the direct vicinity of the geopolitical fold-lines of the region. Moreover, South-Eastern Europe is a litmus test for the capacities of a truly European foreign policy. Finally, the OSCE is a particularly apt framework within which to organise endeavours to address the root causes of the past and present conflicts. Following are a few remarks about the Stability Pact and the different countries concerned.

Stability Pact

The Stability Pact for South-Eastern Europe is placed under the auspices of the OSCE due to its field Presence in most of the States of this region. We have to keep up the momentum, while at the same time avoiding creating too-high expectations on the part of the countries of South-Eastern Europe. The Stability Pact should not be a new superstructure, but a catalyst through which the various international organisations involved act according to their comparative advantages. The OSCE has an in-depth knowledge of the region, which it is making use of. Austria intends to contribute to some dimensions, such as children in armed conflicts, the strengthening of the rule of law and gender issues.

Croatia

The new 'macro-political' approach of the OSCE Mission towards this country is a positive one, but until now it has not produced the expected results. Some improvements have been made to the electoral law under pressure from the international community, but the choice of the date for the parliamentary elections represented another backlash. It remains to be seen whether the situation after these elections will be more conducive to a *rapprochement* to Western Europe. In any case, the extension of the mandate of the OSCE Mission to Croatia is essential.

Bosnia and Herzegovina

Austria supports the 'local ownership' approach developed by High Representative Wolfgang Petritsch. This includes more self-reliance on local and regional bodies while maintaining a firm stance towards those who torpedo the Dayton Peace Agreement. We are therefore also supportive of the decision to bar a number of parties from participating in the April 2000 municipal elections – which will be another primary challenge for Austria and the OSCE. The OSCE Mission to Bosnia and Herzegovina plays a major role in the implementation process, somehow adding flesh to the skeleton provided for by the Dayton Agreement.

Kosovo

The OSCE Mission has to build up structures from the grass-roots level and to address the structural causes of the conflict. Despite all the difficulties it is facing, the Mission has already achieved a lot. The establishment of a Police School can be seen as a first success, especially since multi-ethnicity is maintained among the cadets. The training of Kosovar local administrators is currently under way, based on a co-operative model and promoted by the Mission. Training (and licensing) is also taking place for journalists and more generally the media. But of course, the most important issue remains the organisation of elections. Austria favours the holding of local elections that would help to stabilise the existing local administrations and to increase the existing co-operation between them and UNMIK. However, those elections should only occur after a careful preparation. In this respect, it is essential to have a UN civil registry as soon as possible.

Montenegro

Here is another touchstone of the OSCE's activities in the region. Austria supports the work of the ODHIR office in Podgorica. Within the framework of the European Union, we are pushing for increased funding of Montenegrin economic reforms.

The question of a readmission of the Federal Republic of Yugoslavia within the OSCE might come up, but can only be considered after the current regime in

Belgrade has fallen and free and fair elections are held. A new Yugoslav government must unequivocally commit itself to all OSCE norms and standards.

Albania

The OSCE has achieved a great deal in Albania. It is partly due to the efforts undertaken by the international community through the OSCE framework to stabilise Albania in recent years, such as legal reforms and police laws. Austria intends to boost the 'Friends of Albania' Group, which proved an effective framework through which to co-ordinate international activities. Austria foresees a high-level Friends of Albania meeting in Vienna which has been tentatively scheduled for 28 January 2000.

The Former Yugoslav Republic of Macedonia

This country has endured great hardship during the Kosovo crisis. The OSCE helps to balance inter-ethnic relations. The Mission is doing a great job in this regard.

Conclusion

The OSCE makes a critical contribution to the long-term pacification of the Balkans. It has comparative advantages which have to be exploited as much as possible.

PART I
THE OPERATIONAL ACTIVITIES OF THE OSCE IN SOUTH-EASTERN EUROPE

PART I

Chapter 1

A Success Story: The United Nations Transitional Authority for Eastern Slavonia

Willy Hanset

Firstly I would like to thank the organisers of the international conference of which this volume is the Proceedings for having invited me. This opportunity, this privilege, allows me to present the immense work done by our 'Blue Helmets' in Eastern Slavonia.

My chapter will treat three principal themes: a short historical summary, the UNTAES Mission and some historical lessons which explain the Mission's success. I will be writing from personal experience.

The Yugoslav Crisis: Short Historical Summary

In June 1991 the Yugoslav crisis erupted on to the international scene. Slovenia and Croatia claimed their independence while the Serb population, minority but certainly present, remained loyal to the federal power. Croatia and Slovenia were rapidly shaken by violent fighting. The Federal Army under Serb control, guarantor of Federal unity and identity, remained in its barracks in the heart of the dissident regions. Soon, Yugoslav troops invaded the new States to support the Serbs who refused to accept the division. In January 1992 Croatia and Slovenia were officially recognised by the European community and in March by the United States. Also in March, the first Blue Helmets arrived, dispatched by the United Nations to ensure that the ceasefire was respected, and peace maintained.

In Eastern Slavonia, it was Russian and Belgian soldiers who from March 1992 to January 1996 handled, both well and badly, this difficult mission. They belonged to the United Nations Protection Force, UNPROFOR, deployed throughout the territory of the former Yugoslavia. In May and August 1995, Croat armed forces launched operations 'Flash' and 'Storm' recapturing all the territory under Serb control, except for Eastern Slavonia. The Croat authorities and the Serb leadership started peace negotiations, which ended with the signature on the 12 November 1995 of the Erdut accord.

The Erdut Accord

This basic agreement, brokered and stewarded by American Ambassador Peter W. Galbraith and the United Nations mediator Thorvald Stoltenberg was signed at Erdut on 12 November 1995 by Milan Milanovic, head of the Serb delegation, and by Hrvoje Sarinic, head of the Croat delegation. The signatories to the accord agreed among other things:

– That a transitional period of twelve months would be established, which could be extended for a further twelve months at the demand of one of the parties.
– That the UN Security Council would put in place a transitional administration charged with governing the region in the interest of all the persons residing in or returning to it.
– That the Security Council authorise the deployment of a multi-national force during the transitional period to maintain peace and security. The region was to be demilitarised not later than thirty days after the force was declared operational. This demilitarisation was to effect all the military forces and the police and above all apply to the weapons present in the region.
– That the transitional administration would ensure that refugees and displaced persons could in complete security return to their homes. The transitional administration was to take all necessary measures for the re-establishment and normal functioning of public services.
– That a transitional police force would be established under the control of the transitional administration.

To summarise, this accord foresaw the progressive and peaceful return of the region to Croat rule, underlined the importance of respect for the rights of the people involved, and imposed the holding of elections at the latest thirty days before the end of the transitional period.

UNTAES

Based on the Erdut Accord, the UN Security Council on 15 January 1996 unanimously created UNTAES with resolution 1037:

The Security Council

1. Decides that the military component of UNTAES shall consist of a force with an initial deployment of up to 5,000 troops which will have the following mandate:

(a) To supervise and facilitate the demilitarisation as undertaken by the parties to the Basic Agreement, according to the schedule and procedures to be established by UNTAES;

(b) To monitor the voluntary and safe return of refugees and displaced persons to their home of origin in co-operation with the United Nations High Commissioner for Refugees, as provided for in the Basic Agreement;

(c) To contribute, by its presence, to the maintenance of peace and security in the region; and

(d) Otherwise to assist in implementation of the Basic Agreement.

2. Decides that Member States, acting nationally or through regional organisations or arrangements, may, at the request of UNTAES and on the basis of procedures communicated to the United Nations, take all necessary measures, including close air support, in defence of UNTAES and, as appropriate, to assist in the withdrawal of UNTAES;

3. Reaffirms that all States shall co-operate fully with the International Tribunal for the Former Yugoslavia and its organs in accordance with the provisions of resolution 827 (1993) of 25 May 1993 and the Statute of the International Tribunal and shall comply with requests for assistance or orders issued by a Trial Chamber under article 29 of the Statute;

4. Stresses that UNTAES shall co-operate with the International Tribunal in the performance of its mandate, including with regard to the protection of the sites identified by the Prosecutor and persons conducting investigations for the International Tribunal.

A Strong Mandate

The mandate defined by the Security Council is strong because it rests on Chapter VII of the UN Charter which authorises the use of force, not only in the case of legitimate defence but also for the execution of a mandated mission.

This strong mandate was given added credibility by UNTAES's military component which included 5,000 men, later joined by more than a hundred military observers. A credibility reinforced by the weapons at the Force Commander's disposition: two artillery batteries, and two squadrons of tanks. A firepower further reinforced by the presence of six combat helicopters under the direct command of the Force Commander. Finally, if ever needed the Force Commander could call upon Close Air Support from NATO planes deployed to support IFOR troops in Bosnia and Herzegovina. The Force Commander had this authority and all that was logistically necessary for this support was already present within the theatre of the operation. Full-scale training exercises were organised two or three times per week. A strong mandate, supported by a credible force was a major asset for the Force Commander whose mission, put differently, was to reintegrate Eastern Slavonia into the Croatian State, while maintaining its multi-ethnic character and ensuring respect for minorities and more generally the rights of all.

UNTAES 1996: Demilitarisation

The military component of UNTAES attained two important stages in 1996 led by the Belgian Force Commander Major General Schoups. Based on the two units of Blue Helmets already in place, the Belgian and Russian battalions, the Force Commander by the beginning of May was up to full strength with an operational force of 5,000 men including a Belgian battalion reinforced by an Argentine reconnaissance company, a Russian battalion, a group of Pakistani forces, a group of Jordanian forces, a squadron of Ukrainian tanks, a squadron of Ukrainian helicopters, a Slovaque engineering corps, an Indonesian medical company, a Czech field hospital, a group of Polish police and a Headquarters company provided by Belgium.

The demilitarisation of the zone started on 26 May and by 26 July the demilitarisation was completed and respected by the two parties. Only UNTAES soldiers controlled the zone and they secured it by occupying all the points controlling access and by patrolling night and day in all the villages and conurbations. An important de-mining effort was undertaken. A 'security and logistics' support was brought to a series of projects developed by the civil elements of UNTAES. Let me mention, just by way of example, that on 1 November, 500 people were authorised to return to the cemeteries to celebrate in dignity All Saints' Day. Step by step Serbs and Croats relearned how to meet, talk and help each other; but the road to refound confidence remains a long one.

UNTAES 1997: *en route* for Success

I once again took command of UNTAES on 6 January 1997. At that time everyone was conscious of the determination of the UN. The work of UNTAES was having its effects from day to day: the opening of a school, a market being set up, checkpoints opening. As foreseen by Security Council resolution 1037, UNTAES was to organise elections and rubber-stamp the result.

These elections were to take place on 13 and 14 April 1997. They were a success for the UN and for UNTAES. In spite of serious organisational problems the elections passed off without a single incident, not a shot fired, not even a punch-up. Everybody recognised that the reason these elections were able to take place was thanks to the extraordinary security effort of the Blue Helmets. They gave of their best. For a whole week both night and day 4,000 Blue Helmets were deployed on the ground in three concentric circles of security. The first circle was made up of checkpoints and observation posts installed on the edges of the region and controlling all entry points to the zone. At these checkpoints strict control stopped the introduction of arms into the zone and refused entry to troublemakers. The second circle, composed of checkpoints was inside the zone. On all roads leading to the polling stations and the ballot paper collection points, patrols and mobile checkpoints dissuaded any disruptive actions. Finally, the third circle was a discreet but real presence of intervention forces installed in the vicinity of the polling stations. Under the orders of the Force Commander, a mobile (by helicopter and by road) specialised intervention force stood by, ready to intervene anywhere in the zone.

Order and security in the polling stations themselves was the responsibility of the Transitional Police. The one hundred military observers, unarmed, were in the polling stations and continually updated the Force Commander on how things were evolving, and the electoral mood. This security presence and also the extra logistic support supplied by the military allowed the elections to take place.

In his report to the Security Council the Secretary-General of the UN, Kofi Annan, underlined that 'the success of the local elections of 13 April mark an important stage in the process aimed at giving the local population a legitimate representation'.

The elections marked a point of no return in the process of reintegration of Eastern Slavonia into the Croatian State. The military, the Blue Helmets of UNTAES played a fundamental role in this, and I pay homage to them.

At the request of UNTAES the office of the OSCE in charge of Democratic Institutions and Human Rights (ODIHR) sent observers to check the correct execution of the elections of 13 and 14 April 1997. The mandate of these OSCE teams was simply to observe, not to supervise nor to certify the elections. The certification was the responsibility of the transitional administrator of UNTAES, Mr Klein.

Since mid-February 1997, twenty-two OSCE long-term observers had been deployed in ten different places in Croatia, including in UNTAES's area of responsibility. Its worth noting that the 192 OSCE observers (ODIHR) were deployed on election day throughout the Croat territory, including UNTAES's zone.

After the elections, while the new elected bodies were having trouble getting set up, it appeared that the next challenge which faced UNTAES would be the return of refugees. The local Serbs had shown that they were resolved to assume their rights and responsibilities as Croat citizens but there remained in the region a feeling of distrust, even of fear. The moment came to cut the lifeline which linked Eastern Slavonia with Serbia and to reintegrate the region within the Croat system. For example, and without being exhaustive, I could mention public services such as the post, justice, teaching, public health, the pensions system, the railways and the prison system, and the introduction of the kuna instead of the dinar. The refugees would only return on the condition that they had somewhere to stay, to send their children to school, and to work. The reactivation of the region was essentially led by the civil branch of UNTAES with logistic support from the military part at a strength of 5,000 men from twenty-two different nations.

During this period which lasted from May until October 1997, the military force transferred progressively and with great caution a part of its power to the Transitional Police Force (TPF) which was undergoing training. This was the period of peaceful co-existence. In order to avoid an everlasting deployment, following a scenario 'a la Cypriot' but above all because the essential objectives of the mandate had been attained, UNTAES planned a two-stage pull-out strategy. During the first stage, the transitional administration was to transfer to Croatia the responsibility for the majority of civil administration of the region, while guarding the right to intervene. During the second stage, depending on progressive results, the last administrative functions (particularly police functions) were in turn transferred to Croatia. On the military side, a plan of progressive disengagement was elaborated.

On 14 July 1997, with resolution 1120, the Security Council prolonged UNTAES's mandate until 15 January 1998 and authorised the execution of the plan for military withdrawal. During August the Pakistani, Jordanian, and Argentinean Blue Helmets went home. This reduction by half of men and heavy weapons obliged the Force Commander to redeploy the Belgian and Russian battalions. Who, ironically, were back to their original deployment in the former Eastern sector.

At the same time, the security system, until then based on fixed checkpoints evolved into an essentially mobile system: the control of entry being gradually passed to the Transitional Police guided and watched by the civil UN police.

On 15 October the number of men was again reduced, and a residual force of 720 men was installed charged with 'liquidating' the mission. From this date the sole mission of these soldiers was to assure, if needed, the security of UN personnel and to guard the materials and equipment belonging to the organisation.

On 15 January 1998, complete authority for the region was transferred to the Croat Government: the mandate was completed. Eastern Slavonia was returned peacefully to the Croatian fold. The region has kept her multi-ethnic character. With their presence, their determination and their professionalism, UNTAES's Blue Helmets were the framework around which all of UNTAES's civil action could develop and consolidate. This was my extraordinary experience at the head of UNTAES's Blue Helmets during 1997.

Conclusion

The UNTAES operation was considered a success by everyone. The principal objectives imposed by the Security Council on the transitional administration were attained. The military component of UNTAES realised all its objectives. Two essential tasks remain to be completed: to organise a dignified return for the refugees and to handle with generosity the displaced persons. It is the Croat State which is now responsible for this. It is up to the Croats to reconcile the different populations in Eastern Slavonia. Then, and only then, will UNTAES have been a real success.

For the moment the factors which allowed the success of the military operation can be identified as the following:

- A mandate which clearly defined the civil and military objectives while remaining sufficiently general. It covered all the situations encountered on the ground, giving military action an official legitimacy.
- The reference in the mandate to Chapter VII of the UN Charter which allowed the development of solid rules of engagement: it was the price of UNTAES's credibility.
- A credible military component: 5,000 men equipped with their armaments, and able to count on the close aerial support of NATO planes.
- A simple chain of command, clear and short. All decisions were taken by the Transitional Administrator and the Force Commander.
- The decisional process was rapid and reacted directly according to developments on the ground. The situation was not aggravated.
- The presence of a hundred military observers deployed in all the region's villages. They were the 'eyes and ears' of the Force Commander.
- Excellent co-ordination with all the humanitarian organisations, logistic efficiency and efficient de-mining teams were also assets.

In order to achieve a full reconciliation between the individuals who had become embroiled in the war, the UN decided to maintain a Support Group of

Civil Police in Eastern Slavonia for a period of nine months. At the request of Croatia, the OSCE will return to the region to ensure that the signed accords between the Croat Government and UNTAES are put into action. This will allow the UN to withdraw, while ensuring that the enormous work realised by the international community is consolidated. Already, before the end of its mandate UNTAES co-operated closely with the members of the OSCE to ensure a smooth transition.

Whatever the future holds in this magnificent region of the Danube that is Eastern Slavonia, we must pay our respects to the gigantic achievement of all the Blue Helmets. We should bow before all those who gave their lives or suffered bodily.

Chapter 2

Croatia: Status Report

Bernard Poncet

As an introduction, I will begin with a short review of the most recent political events in Croatia. I will then present the general activities of the Mission and its preliminary conclusions regarding progress made by the Government in fulfilling its international commitments in recent months and conclude with an update on the forthcoming parliamentary elections.

Introduction

Croatia today is a country in transition in several respects. Croatia is confronted with a process of post-conflict normalisation, as well as the transition from socialism to democracy. The upcoming elections for the Lower House of the Croatian Parliament, which have been called for Monday 3 January 2000, present the possibility of another transition: political. For the first time since independence, the dominance of the party in power, the Croatian Democratic Union (HDZ), and its charismatic leader, Dr Franjo Tudjman, who has led the country since 1990, are questioned at the national level. Indeed, the parliamentary elections may result in the first democratic transfer of power in independent Croatia.

However, due to the illness of the President, and the constitutional dilemma his incapacitation has caused, the country is not yet in the mood of an election campaign. President Tudjman has been in hospital for over one month. His medical team has described his condition most recently as 'very grave'. The uncertainty about his health has fuelled all sorts of speculation about his capacity to govern and raised the question of the proper constitutional resolution of the succession question. Most notably, the President has failed to call the elections for 22 December 1999 as previously planned, but the Government and HDZ officials insisted that he was not 'permanently prevented' from performing his duties. They refused opposition calls to implement article 97 of the Croatian Constitution, which states that the Speaker of Parliament takes over for sixty days, until Presidential elections are held, in case of the President's death, resignation or permanent incapacitation.

Instead of triggering the constitutional mechanism on 'permanent incapacitation', the HDZ successfully pushed for passage in Parliament of a Constitutional Law regulating the President's 'temporary' inability to fulfil his functions. Parliament met on 24 November after a two-week pause and passed the Constitutional Law. This followed several days of extensive consultations between the HDZ and opposition parties. Still, attempts to reach consensus on the Constitutional Law with the six mainstream parties known as the 'Opposition Six' failed. The HDZ was able to muster the eighty-five votes necessary to pass the Constitutional Law only with the support of several right-wing and fringe parties, as well as with the votes of certain independent and minority candidates (although the governing party presently holds a clear majority in the Lower House of Parliament, it does not indeed have the two-thirds majority necessary to pass constitutional laws or amendments).

The 'temporary' incapacity of the President was determined by the Constitutional Court at the request of the Government and will last sixty days, after which it can be extended, meaning that the Speaker of the House, Dr. Vlatko Pavlevic, will fulfil presidential functions as long as President Tudjman is unable to do so. Finally according to the terms of the new Constitutional Law, it was the Speaker of Parliament D. Pavlevic who called parliamentary elections immediately after having been proclaimed acting President.

Mission Mandate and Activities

Based on a rather broad mandate of April 1996, the Mission monitors the Government's progress in meeting the numerous commitments it has undertaken, for example upon Croatia's accession to the Council of Europe in 1996, regarding the return of refugees and displaced persons, human rights and rights of national minorities, integration of the Danube Region and democratisation, including media and election reform. These international obligations and commitments undertaken by Croatia over the course of the past few years in order to move closer to Euro-Atlantic structures form the terms of reference for the exercise of the Mission's 'monitoring, advice and assistance' role in the country.

The Mission monitors these commitments, advises and assists in their fulfilment, and reports on the issues in Weekly Reports and four-monthly Progress Reports. The Mission's regular Weekly Report is an operational document that among other things serves as an 'early warning system' for the Government on areas of concern for the Mission. The Weekly Reports form the basis for the Progress Reports. These reports do not describe the 'current state of affairs' in the country, but assess the progress of the Government of the Republic of Croatia in fulfilling its international obligations and commitments during the reporting period.

In its latest, fifth Progress Report issued on 28 September 1999, and subsequently presented to the Permanent Council, the Mission concluded that there had been piecemeal progress in some areas covered in the Mission's mandate. In the most important areas however, no substantial progress had been made in the preceding four-month period. Four areas have been identified repeatedly by the Mission as priorities for the Government:

- repossession of property (by returning refugees and displaced persons, especially Croatian Serbs);
- the clear and transparent implementation of the Amnesty Law, coupled with the correct and impartial pursuit of war crimes cases in domestic courts (which also affects the return of ethnic Serbs and their faith in Croatian authorities);
- full co-operation with the International Criminal Tribunal for the Former Yugoslavia (ICTY);
- the proceeding of applications for naturalisation and verification of citizenship.

The Mission also noted in its last Progress Report that, one and a half years after the formal post-conflict integration of Croatia, discriminatory laws introduced as temporary emergency measures during the conflict remain in force, perpetuating divisions within the society. Still, the security situation in most of the war-affected areas was reported to be satisfactory with a decreasing number of reported incidents. An exception was the area around the town of Vukovar, where a notable increase in the number of ethnically-related incidents was seen. Incidents escalated when not addressed by the authorities and culminated in the killing of an ethnic Serb in the village of Berak in August 1999. Finally, in view of the forthcoming parliamentary elections, the continued lack of progress in the areas of electoral and media reform was and remains of particular concern to the Mission.

Perhaps the most time- and labour-intensive Mission activity involves monitoring of the Government's implementation of commitments related to the return and reintegration of refugees and displaced persons. More than half a million people were forced to flee their homes during the course of the 1991–95 armed conflict in Croatia. The Mission monitors the implementation of Government commitments in co-operation with the UN High Commissioner for Refugees (UNHCR) and the European Community Monitor Mission (ECMM) and works closely with the authorities on central and local levels, providing assistance and advice whenever problems are identified.

In June 1998, the Croatian Parliament approved a Government programme for the return of refugees which recognises the inalienable right of all Croatian citizens to return, promises equal treatment and establishes procedures for repossession of temporarily occupied property. Security is not a major issue for returnees, and the physical return of refugees now appears to be well organised. Procedures for return are in place, although many administrative hurdles must be negotiated by potential refugees. But repossession of property and the reconstruction process, especially involving Croatian citizens of Serb ethnicity, are highly problematic. The Mission still has major concerns with regards to the legal framework for the provision of equal rights to all Croatian citizens, particularly returning Serbs. These citizens are still discriminated against in law with regard to repossession of occupied property, reconstruction of destroyed property, and access to benefits, particularly for so-called 'self-assisted' returnees. Although initiatives taken by the Government during the summer of 1999 have improved the framework and systems supporting the process of return, a number of problems remain.

The Mission makes a positive assessment of return movements which continued throughout the Kosovo crisis and continue now. It has to be pointed out that according to UNHCR statistics from 1 January 1999 till mid-November, approximately 32,000 people were able to return to their places of origin, this including returns from and to the Danube region as well as returns to Croatia from FRY, Bosnia and Herzegovina and other countries.

The Mission remains concerned over provisions which continue to discriminate against individuals in the Law on Reconstruction and the Law on Areas of Special State Concern. It also remains concerned by the evidence of the non-applicability of the Return Programme in the Danube Region and the use of the courts system generally by ethnic Croat returnees to repossess property in the Danube Region. A number of mainly ethnic Serb displaced persons in the Danube Region have been evicted from their places of temporary occupancy on the basis of the law rather than the Programme, and thus without the provision of any form of alternative accommodation by the Government.

To provide assistance to the Government in identifying core problems with the physical implementation of the Return Programme, the Mission and the UNHCR now present the Government with monthly assessments of the performance of local authorities on, in particular, repossession of property.

The protection of Human Rights and the rights of national minorities is a primary focus of the mandate of the Mission and a key element in the building of trust, the rule of law and the proper functioning of democratic institutions and processes. Consequently, the Mission analyses draft legislation and other types of governmental acts for their conformity with the international human rights norms established under the international human rights instruments to which Croatia is a party, primarily the European Convention on Human Rights. In this context, the Mission works closely with the OSCE High Commissioner on National Minorities, who visited Croatia again a few weeks ago, as well as with the Council of Europe.

In general, the Government has made little progress in meeting long-standing obligations with regard to amending or abolishing certain laws. In particular, the 1991 Constitutional Law on Human Rights and Freedoms and Rights of Ethnic and National Communities or Minorities, whose suspended provisions the Government undertook to amend in 1996 remain in force, as well as return-related laws mentioned earlier. Other laws that have been amended, for example the Law on Local Government and Self-Government, have not been promulgated or published, rendering them inaccessible to the public and impossible to assess.

Unlike the previous Electoral Law, the October 1999 Electoral Law no longer requires all candidates to identify their ethnicity. However, it has retained provisions requiring the identification of ethnicity of any candidate proposed by 100 or more voters.

An important element in the Mission's mandate is the reintegration into Croatian society of individuals, institutions and public services in the formerly Serb-controlled areas. Of particular relevance for the Danube Region are the thirty-two agreements that the Government made with the United Nations Transitional Administration (UNTAES) during the period of the region's peaceful reintegration from 1996 to 1998. The Mission pays particular attention to the 1997 Amnesty Law, where clarity and transparency are still lacking, and to procedures related to the prosecution of individuals for war crimes committed during the armed conflict in Croatia. The Mission recommends that war crime prosecution be pursued in a manner consistent with Croatia's international obligations and in close co-operation with the ICTY.

In Croatia, the OSCE has for the first time undertaken the role of monitoring local police authorities through the Police Monitoring Group in the Danube Region. The Mission took over these responsibilities from the United Nations in late 1998. The Mission's co-operation with the local police force has been very good, based on professionalism on both sides. In order to increase their professional skills, the OSCE has facilitated and financed a training seminar for Croatian policemen at the Italian Police Academy in Rome last summer.

The Government has basically complied with the agreements with UNTAES regarding the integration of public employees and its obligations in minority education and health care.

The issue of missing persons remains fraught with emotions. A positive step was taken regarding the Danube Region Sub-Commission for Missing Persons when two Serb members were officially appointed, which hopefully will encourage Serb co-operation to locate missing persons and help ease tensions.

Regarding domestic war crimes prosecution, the successful appeal of 24 November to the Supreme Court of the so-called Sodolovci group was an encouraging step. The five Serb indictees had been convicted earlier this year by the regional court in Osijek to serve long-term sentences because they were supposedly present at the village of Sodolovci when Serb military units based there shelled a Croatian village during the armed conflict. Concerns remain regarding impartial war crimes prosecution, as a number of recent returnees of Serb ethnicity were arrested. Ongoing war crimes trials leave uncertainties about the quality of evidence and whether old indictments are being used. *In absentia* trials for war crimes still take place.

The Government has hardened its stance regarding ICTY jurisdiction over operations 'Flash' and 'Storm' in 1995, recently denying on-site investigations. Peripheral documents were lately submitted to the Hague Tribunal.

The overall security situation in the Danube Region is currently reported as stable, but the economic outlook remains bleak, posing a limit to Croat return and a disincentive for Serbs to remain.

One of the Mission's key areas is the freedom of the media. Since independence, the Government has committed itself to uphold democratic standards in that field. The Mission's four-monthly progress reports have pointed out the Government's failure to fulfil this obligation, in particular in the area of electronic media.

Some improvements in the news programming of Croatian Television (HTV) have been noted over recent years. In particular, instances of inflammatory speech have been reduced, and the access of opposition parties to television has increased. Nevertheless, international monitoring of news and current affairs coverage on HTV over recent months reveal a continuous pattern of unbalanced news programming in favour of the ruling party. While some effort to achieve more balance in reporting of party activities has been apparent since October, it has been inconsistent.

A particular problem is that figures of the ruling party, especially when appearing in their capacity as government or state officials as opposed to their party capacity, continue to receive an overwhelmingly disproportionate amount of coverage.

The political bias, apparent in HTV's programming, is linked with shortcomings in the legislative framework that governs Croatian Radio-Television (HRT). The HRT Law fails to provide the State television with the institutional independence that would protect it from political direction. Amendments to the Law in October 1998 ignored most of the recommendations made by the Council of Europe experts earlier that year, and thus failed to achieve the Government's stated objective of transforming HRT into a public broadcaster. According to the agreement reached between the ruling party and the main opposition grouping in May 1999, the HRT Law was supposed to be amended again before the forthcoming parliamentary election, in order to transform it into a public service broadcaster. However, the parties were subsequently unable to reach agreement on such amendments and the country enters the election campaign with the Law unchanged.

A positive step being taken in the area of private media is the setting up of a network of private television broadcasters around the country, which will share news programming. This will provide the majority of television viewers with a diversity of choice which has until now been lacking. However, there has been no progress in privatising the third channel of HTV, as recommended by the international community. While a concession for a new, private fourth channel was granted earlier this year, it appears that the October deadline for formally signing the concession agreement has not been met.

Regarding the print media, the unresolved financial difficulties of the near-monopoly press distribution company, Tisak, continue to place strains on publishers. A rehabilitation plan, involving the takeover of Tisak by a consortium of State-owned banks in April 1999, has not resolved these difficulties, and independent media remain vulnerable.

Elections

Let us now turn to the election issue, which is currently among the most interesting points. Participating States of the OSCE are obliged to guarantee that elections are universal and equal, fair and free, transparent and accountable. In this context, the President of Croatia signed a document in 1996 upon Croatia's accession to the Council of Europe, stating that his country will 'comply, well before the elections, with the recommendations made by the election observers of the Council of Europe and other organisations, in particular with regard to the special voting block for the Diaspora, minority representation, voter registration lists, voter anonymity, the need to increase the independence of the state broadcasting corporation (HRT) and to undertake a census of the population as soon as possible'. More or less the same issues were addressed in the recommendations of the OSCE/ODIHR Election Observation Mission for the Croatian presidential elections of 1997, highlighting the need for independent media, multi-party participation in the electoral commissions, election monitoring by local non-partisan observers, transparency of campaign financing and last but not least, the enfranchisement of all individuals with the right to Croatian citizenship.

These were the benchmarks for the Mission's discussions with the authorities in Croatia on the issue of electoral reform. The Mission, along with partners in the international community, has made very clear through a constant dialogue with the Government that it expects that Croatia will honour its commitments. As early as August 1998, the views of the international community on electoral reform were communicated to the Government in the form of a non-paper, and reiterated in various ways over the succeeding fifteen months with the parliamentary elections in 1999/2000 in mind.

The goal in this endeavour was to provide the authorities with the advice and assistance that would ultimately lead to an assessment of the upcoming elections as 'free and fair'.

In the final analysis, some recommendations of the international community were taken into account in the recently-adopted electoral legislation. The Mission welcomed, for example, that the fixed number of seats for Croatian citizens living permanently abroad (the so-called 'Diaspora') was replaced by a non-fixed quota; that domestic non-partisan observation of the elections was made possible for the first time, and that the electoral commissions will be composed of members of several parties. The Mission hopes that the newly-established Election Ethical Commission will also have a positive influence, in particular during the campaign period.

That said, international concerns regarding other important issues affecting elections – reform of State television, reform of disputed citizenship legislation, treatment of minority representation, transparency in campaign financing, publication of voters' lists and so on – remain unchanged. Due to the late adoption of the electoral legislation, the necessary framework for full and proper implementation of the law and related procedures may not be completely in place by Election Day.

However, I must stress that the assessment of the electoral process, including the legislation, the campaign, and the election administration, will not be made by the Mission, but by the OSCE Office for Democratic Institutions and Human Rights (ODIHR).

Following previous practice, ODIHR has established an Election Observation Mission that will monitor the elections on 3 January 2000, as it did for the Croatian parliamentary elections in 1995, as well as the presidential elections in 1997. The OSCE and other international organisations have been invited by the Croatian Government to observe the upcoming elections. Regarding the involvement of the OSCE, there is a clear distinction and division of responsibilities between the long-term Mission to Croatia and the ODIHR Election Observation Mission.

As it stands now, approximately twenty long-term observers will be deployed throughout Croatia. Long-term observers from various participating States have already been deployed in Croatia during the last two weeks. Their role is to acquire first-hand knowledge about the effectiveness and impartiality of the pre-election administration, the implementation of the election law and related regulations, the nature of the campaign and the political environment prior to voting day. Approximately three or four days before the polling day, short-term observers, perhaps as many as 200, will come to Croatia. They will monitor the actual voting in the polling stations. Within 24 hours after closing of the vote, the ODIHR Mission will issue a preliminary statement on the conduct of the elections. A detailed report is usually presented to the public about one month later.

The Mission, of course, hopes that this analysis will come to the conclusion that the parliamentary elections in Croatia were 'free and fair'.

The Mission has nevertheless certain concerns with regard to the date, although it is clear that determining such a date is the prerogative of the President (or in this case, the acting President) and a matter of sovereignty. First of all, as the Mission has repeatedly stated, the holding of elections during the late December to early January holiday period is extremely unusual in European practice. Second, the choice of 3 January 2000 does not reflect a domestic political consensus. The Acting President called the election so quickly after the HDZ Presidency made the decision on the date that there was no attempt to take into consideration the views of other parties, which have severely criticised this date. Thirdly, it should be pointed that out-of-country voting, for example in Bosnia and Herzegovina, will take place on 2 and 3 January 2000. Holding elections only one or two days after the New Year is certain to make international monitoring efforts much more difficult and complicated, casting strong doubts about the sincerity of the authorities' proclaimed eagerness to have international observers monitor the electoral process. Furthermore, the election campaign period will be shortened due to the observance of the Christmas Holidays in heavily Roman Catholic Croatia. Finally, proper election administration may also be affected by the proximity of elections to the New Year holiday. This is to say nothing of possible problems –

such as disruption of travel and flight schedules – related to the 'Y2K' computer problems.

In short, it seems that few people outside the governing HDZ party are very happy about the election date. And the health of President Tudjman adds an element of uncertainty to the election and campaign preparations.

In any case, the upcoming elections will be the decisive yardstick Croatia will be measured against, when it comes to pursuing her strategic goal of closer integration into Euro-Atlantic structures. The Mission stands ready to assist the new Government, whatever its composition, on this path.

Chapter 3

Bosnia and Herzegovina: Status Report

Robert L. Barry

As the year ends, considerable rhetorical progress has been made on the agenda for peace in Bosnia and Herzegovina (BiH). The New York Declaration and the statement by President Jelavic at the Istanbul Summit contain important commitments on strengthening central institutions, return of refugees and displaced persons, a joint border service, military reductions and integration, economic reform and regional co-operation. Translating these commitments into reality will be a challenge, as was immediately apparent from the criticisms levelled at the New York Declaration by both entities (the Federation of Bosnia and Herzegovina and the Republika Srpska).

The arrival of High Representative Petritsch and the priorities he has set have resulted in closer co-operation within the international community and more decisive joint action. Our highest priority is the return of displaced persons, and an early step was to harmonise property laws in the two entities and insist on their implementation. This required that elected leaders take responsibility for their own country's promises to reverse the trend towards dependency, but to make this work it has been necessary to take firm action against obstructionists. Two recalcitrant Serb parties – the Radicals and the SSRS – in effect eliminated themselves from the 2000 elections by refusing to drop officers such as Nikola Poplasen who had already been removed from office for failure to abide by the General Framework Agreement for Peace. The removal of twenty-two obstructionist officials, linked to the statement in the New York Declaration that there could be no place in BiH for those who obstruct the peace process and spread hate and ethnic enmity, has been widely welcomed by the public. The individuals concerned, local strong men, will not go willingly – but their political careers are effectively ended as they will not be able to hold elected or appointed office in 2000.

Against this backdrop of the fourth anniversary of Dayton and the New York Declaration, a great deal has happened since Ambassador Dieter Woltmann last reported to the Permanent Council on 26 August 1999. Some of the most significant developments are given below.

The draft election law was completed and sent to the BiH Parliament for action on 10 November 1999. This is a major contribution to the democratisation process of Bosnia. The elected leaders of the country should act with urgency in passing the election law as it is imperative not only for Bosnia and Herzegovina's integration into Europe, but also to give hope to the people of BiH that their political system will continue to function once the international community leaves. Several hearings have been held, and while there has been considerable criticism of the law's provisions we continue to hope that the BiH Parliament will adopt the law in February 2000.

The Election Law Information Campaign continues its efforts to educate the BiH public about the draft law. Round table discussions and meetings on the draft are continuing at the grass-roots level. Daily TV and radio public service announcements about the election law are being broadcast on the four major television networks and on the twenty-five independent radio stations across BiH.

The OSCE has taken the lead on media issues in Bosnia and Herzegovina since a free and fair media without political influence is imperative to a functioning democracy. We are heavily engaged with the BiH media and ensuring its impartiality and professionalism. Among the initiatives we have developed are a 'free media' hotline and an independent radio network. We are preparing media laws and other steps to protect journalists who have been subject to both terrorist attacks and political efforts to silence criticism. We are preparing equitable access guidelines for the upcoming elections, and training political parties in how to use the media.

After considerable delay, the seventeenth session of the Standing Committee on Military Matters (SCMM) – a Dayton institution – met on 3 November to discuss reducing the size of the Federation and Republika Srpska (RS) militaries by 15 per cent by the end of 1999, with another 15 per cent reduction scheduled in the year 2000. Work is also continuing on the creation of a common security policy for all of BiH. The OSCE will continue to stress that military cuts are verifiable and that future SCMMs are conducted at regular intervals.

In conjunction with reducing the entity armies, the OSCE is pushing hard for military integration. This will be a gradual process, as even in the Federation the Croat and Bosniac contingents are at odds with one another. But as shown by the New York Declaration, the concept of integrated units for peacekeeping operations and a State dimension to defence policy is gaining ground.

The OSCE played a major role in the preparation of changes to the property legislation that the High Representative imposed on 27 October. These amendments and instructions bring a greater degree of harmony to the property legislation of the two entities, clarify ambiguities in the law, and set clear procedures for the return of property, and the entitlement to alternative accommodation of those occupying such property.

Since the end of the NATO campaign in Kosovo, refugee and displaced person returns to their homes have accelerated. In particular, returns to the rural Eastern RS, where previously no returns were even expected, began to occur spontaneously. These returns to rural areas highlight an increased sense of security in BiH, and an acceptance of minority returns at the local level. What must be emphasised is that these types of returns could be multiplied, if only funding were flexible. Currently, funding is targeted at certain areas regardless of whether or not return has taken place. The practical result is that we have empty houses sitting in some areas while returnees in other areas try to reconstruct their homes themselves. We need to examine the rigidity of the current funding systems and make sure we can adapt to the needs on the ground.

In urban areas, returns have been admittedly slow. We are beginning, however, to make progress by using Double Occupancy Commissions to break the log-jam in evictions and facilitate information exchange between communities in both entities to advance the return process. Removal of obstructionist housing officials and a ban against elected officials illegally occupying others' housing should accelerate the return process.

Both the party political and coalition registration periods have now been completed for the April 2000 municipal elections and this has resulted in a reduction in the number of coalitions and alliances. The candidate registration period is now in progress, and will remain open until 20 December. Up to 20,000 candidates are expected to register and will be individually validated and screened. Under the new open list system in effect for the municipal elections, candidates' names will be on the ballot papers.

Through its Political Party Development programme, the OSCE continues to support parties that are moderate, democratic and supportive of the Dayton Agreement and a multi-ethnic Bosnia and Herzegovina. The OSCE has provided a series of training workshops for coalition building, efforts to get Bosnian youth engaged in the political process, and help to strategise outreach activities for these moderate parties and in particular their field representatives. All of these activities have been implemented in co-operation with international partner foundations including the National Democratic Institute, the Friedrich Ebert Foundation, and the Friedrich Naumann Foundation.

In order to have a functioning democracy and civil society in BiH and South-Eastern Europe, the role of women in public affairs is crucial. We are undertaking several initiatives to increase levels of women in all fields of public life. One of these initiatives is the Gender Task Force, which comes out of the Stability Pact for South-Eastern Europe. Both the BiH Presidency and the Council of Ministers have been urged by us to officially join the Gender Task Force by nominating an official representative.

The Croatian Parliamentary Elections have been called for 3 January 2000. The OSCE Mission to BiH will assist ODIHR in their effort to observe these elections, in particular the out-of-country voting conducted in BiH. Under Croatian law, as many as 300,000 Bosnian Croats could qualify to vote. We will continue to stress that elections out-of-country should be restricted to official diplomatic and consular representations, that Croatian Serb refugees be allowed to vote, and that we get an accurate number of polling stations to be used for the diaspora in Bosnia.

I believe the vigorous steps taken by OSCE and the international community since our last report to the Permanent Council set the stage for further progress. This next stage is crucial for the future of BiH in Europe, because what is needed now is for the elected officials to take ownership of the peace process and move it along themselves.

Success in Bosnia and Herzegovina will be incomplete if we do not take into account the regional dimension of the problems that we are struggling with here. In my dual role as Special Envoy of the Chairman-in-Office I was charged with making recommendations concerning a regional strategy. That report was made available at the Summit, and I have discussed it informally with delegations. The Istanbul Summit tasked the Permanent Council to develop a regional strategy to support its aims, and I hope my report will be helpful in this process. There is no question that regional co-operation will serve as a catalyst for the integration of the countries of the region into broader structures. At the same time a regional strategy cannot be pursued without resources dedicated to this purpose. While the OSCE cannot be expected to be a major source there must at least be funds available to catalyse contributions from participating states and international organisations. The Stability Pact needs the support that OSCE's field presence can provide, and the field Missions need to be able to at least participate in the planning process.

At the end of my assignment to look at the regional picture, let me share one thought with you. In much of the region, the ruling political parties still control the economic, political and security levers within their countries. Worse, some of the old *nomenklatura* works hand-in-glove with organised crime and the remnants of the security services to retain both political and economic control over the lives of its citizens. This creates a significant threat to internal political stability, not to mention to the political and economic freedoms the people of these countries want. It is deeply troubling to see how, in one of the poorest corners of Europe – and one so dependent on outside aid – many of the political elite have succeeded in enriching themselves. At the same time, the average citizen is forced to struggle to make ends meet because of a late or non-existent salary or pension.

As long as these 'partocracies' exist, the transition to democracy and a market economy will not happen. These nationalist elements have as their top priority the maintenance of the *status quo*. Rule of law, transparency, accountability, true freedom of expression and freedom of the press are all seen as threats to the traditional power base because they dilute party control.

In many transitional economies, the solution to this problem has been found in strict laws on conflict of interest. This means putting sharp limits on political patronage in government, getting the political parties out of the business of appointing judges and influencing the judiciary, and most of all getting elected officials and party representatives off the governing boards of state and municipal enterprises, and keeping them off after privatisation takes place. Such laws could provide real benefits to the people of South-Eastern Europe by encouraging investment, limiting corruption and promoting civil society.

Chapter 4

The Operational Role of the OSCE in the Field of Peace-Building: The Case of Bosnia and Herzegovina

Marianne Ducasse-Rogier

The OSCE Mission to Bosnia and Herzegovina, which was established in December 1995 after the conclusion of the Dayton Peace Agreement, has since been involved in four areas: elections, human rights, democratisation and military stabilisation.[1] Since the main focus of this chapter will be on civil aspects, the last point related to the tasks entrusted to the OSCE by annex 1-B of the peace agreement will be left aside. Nevertheless, I would like to underline that military stabilisation is a very important field of action for any peace-building operation; additionally, it is worth mentioning that the OSCE is probably one of the most suitable organisations to offer its auspices for such activities.

As a general assessment of the state of affairs in Bosnia and Herzegovina today, it could be asserted that despite much improvement since the end of the war (and even since 1996), the situation in this country after four years of peace implementation is still a precarious one in many respects: on the political level, on the economic level, on the institutional (and especially regarding the judiciary) level and of course concerning the return of refugees and displaced persons. The recent dismissal of twenty-two elected and appointed officials by Ambassador Barry, Head of the Mission, and the High Representative Wolfgang Petritsch, illustrates the precariousness of this environment.

Although the OSCE has had a key role to play in the civil implementation of the Dayton Agreement, it would be unfair to hold the Mission solely accountable for this situation. A first reason which can be put forward to support that assertion is an obvious one: many other actors are responsible for the implementation of the Dayton Agreement. As is often pointed out, local actors have a 'primary responsibility' to fulfil their commitments. Additionally, many other international organisations are mandated to participate in the implementation process and very often their activities relate to the same areas as those undertaken by the OSCE

---

[1] The first mandate of the OSCE Mission to Bosnia and Herzegovina was approved in Budapest in December 1995, cf. Decisions of the Budapest Ministerial Council, Decision no. 1, 'OSCE Action for Peace, Democracy and Stability in Bosnia and Herzegovina', 7–8 December 1995, DOC.MC/1/95, 8 December 1995.

Mission (except maybe the supervision of the elections). Among these organisations, the United Nations and the Office of the High Representative (OHR) are especially active, since both of them have seen their field of responsibility increase during the last two years of the peace process.

Another factor downsizing OSCE responsibility for the current situation is that its action derives from a general framework, the Dayton Agreement, which set up key principles for the implementation process. In defining the mandate of the Mission, the OSCE Ministerial Council had thus to take these orientations into account.[2] Likewise, in applying the mandate, the staff of the Mission had to follow the directives set up by the Agreement – as well as those decided by the Peace Implementation Council.[3] Some of these principles may have a very strong impact on the way the activities of the Mission can be fulfilled (for example, the Constitution, which is included in the Dayton Agreement, must be taken into consideration when planning for the elections, as well as when preparing the permanent electoral law).

Finally, the situation in Bosnia and Herzegovina is extremely complex. The conflict which raged between 1992 and 1995 was a terrible one, which left the country in a wrecked state, not least because of ethnic cleansing practices and the subsequent *de facto* partition of the territory. Moreover, the solution brought to that conflict by the Peace Agreement was an ambiguous one. The Dayton Agreement was initially not clear about the nature of the new State which was to be created: the outcome was surprisingly that this State could be considered both as a unitary and a partitioned one.[4] As a consequence, it took time for the international community to develop a coherent strategy aimed at reunifying the country. Additionally, the situation is also complex because Bosnia is not only a war-torn society, but also a country in transition from a socialist-type regime to a democratic one.

Despite these elements, which make it difficult to assess in an isolated way the role of the Mission in Bosnia, I would like to underline some of the problems that specifically undermined OSCE's action and maybe make a few suggestions for current or future operations of this kind in the Balkan region.

---

[2] The duration of the Mission was later on extended by decisions of the OSCE Permanent Council in 1996 (PC.DEC/145, 21 November 1996), 1997 (PC.DEC/203, 11 December 1997) and 1998 (PC.DEC/270, 19 November 1998).

[3] The Peace Implementation Council is a body composed of States and international organisations, which offers political guidance on the implementation of the Dayton Agreement.

[4] Some annexes of the Agreement, such as annex 7 on the return of refugees and displaced persons, favoured the reunification of the State, whereas others, such as annex 1-A on military aspects, were much more ambiguous. The Constitution in itself is a good illustration of that ambiguity: although it underlines that Bosnia remains a unitary State within its internationally recognised borders, the recognition of two entities with extremely large competencies makes it all the more difficult to reunify the country.

Elections

For the OSCE, supervising the first Bosnian general elections in 1996 was a real challenge, for two main reasons. It was the first time that the OSCE was entrusted with such a task, and those elections were extremely complex to organise on both a political and a technical level. The result was in fact imperfect to many observers – and even participants – of the process. As a consequence, many improvements were brought by the OSCE Mission in Bosnia and Herzegovina for the next rounds of elections in 1997 and 1998. Despite these, the 1998 elections were still marred by technical problems (such as the lack of voters' registers in many polling stations on the first day of polling). Nationalist parties are still in power in Bosnia; the institutions do not function properly; Republika Srpska has no President. Moreover, Bosnia is still today without any permanent electoral law, and the OSCE is planning to supervise its fifth electoral round in April 2000 (municipal elections which were scheduled for November 1999 but had to be postponed last summer). The Mission intends to give up supervision only for the next general elections in the course of autumn 2000, which should be held under the permanent electoral law – if it has finally been adopted by then.

To underline some of the issues that relate to this not-so-perfect electoral situation, it is worth coming back to the 1996 elections. The poor achievements of the Mission at the time have influenced the whole electoral process as well as the political life of the country, thus having a strong bearing on the following elections. The main problem was that those first elections occurred too early, when the lack of democratic conditions did not allow for a free and fair process. As a consequence, quite a lot of technical problems occurred. Worse, the political outcome of the election proved detrimental to the peace process: nationalist parties which had started the war acquired a new legitimacy, but remained uncooperative and used their new 'democratic' influence to obstruct the implementation process.

A first factor having contributed to this mistake relates to the way elections were conceived by the negotiators in Dayton: they were regarded as a fundamental starting point for the democratisation of the country.[5] But if a society does not enjoy minimal democratic conditions before elections are organised, it is unlikely that their outcome will be a democratic government. What Bosnia shows is that elections are neither a starting point for democratisation, nor an end in themselves. They should better be considered somewhat as a 'middle point' along the path of a country towards democracy. Therefore, they should only occur after certain conditions have been fulfilled (such as political pluralism, free access to the media and freedom of speech and association).

Another important reason for having early elections in Bosnia, which is more political, related to the obsession of the mandating States with an exit strategy.

---

[5] This conception was not exclusively applied to Bosnia: it also appeared in other peace agreements, and influenced other peace-building operations, such as in Cambodia. Fortunately, it seems that until now at least, the same mistake was not repeated in the case of Kosovo.

Because of the overstated commitments of many of them to withdraw the military force (IFOR at the time) before the end of the year, much pressure was exerted on the Mission to hold those elections before that deadline. Some of those States additionally had other domestic reasons to push for the elections to be held, so that they could present a 'success' on the civilian side of the implementation process, which was starting to appear as the weak link in the Bosnian operation.[6] This pressure was all the more influential as most of the senior staff of the Mission were (and still are) seconded by participating States. Key decision-makers thus happened to be very receptive to the instructions of their own governments.[7]

I mentioned earlier that some positive improvements had been brought by the election branch of the OSCE Mission after the catastrophic 1996 elections. Among them was the decision to launch a general registration operation to update the electoral register, and to have full international supervision of the whole electoral process (including registration, polling and counting). But the most important achievement was of a more political nature, namely the gradual involvement of the OSCE in post-election activities. Especially in the case of municipal elections, for which a certification process was initiated, some pressure began to be exerted on elected officials in order to compel them to respect the results of the elections and to fulfil their mandate in the most democratic way. This practice was later extended, in co-operation with the Office of the High Representative, and offered in extreme cases the possibility to dismiss obstructive officials, granting the international organisations some powers they had previously lacked to overcome deadlocks in the peace process.

Human Rights

Most observers would agree that in Bosnia today a wide range of human rights (be they political or social) are still violated, despite considerable international attention. The Dayton Agreement indeed attached much importance to the issue of human rights and mandated the OSCE regarding them in two ways: the organisation was to support the ombudsman institution created by the Agreement and to monitor and report on the general situation of human rights. Many other organisations were also tasked with monitoring the situation.

Quite quickly frustration appeared with the reporting and monitoring activities, which proved insufficient to improve the situation. It was progressively recognised that Bosnia and Herzegovina was in fact more in need of an huge social and

---

[6] This appears to have particularly been the case for the United States, whose President was at the very same time running for a second mandate and wanted to put forward a successful peace process in Bosnia.

[7] Generally speaking, the question of staff recruitment for the OSCE's field missions seems to be questionable – and indeed is questioned by many: it would be high time for the organisation to develop its own selection procedure instead of relying on the participating States.

political reform to implement and respect the rule of law (that meant that a judicial reform was needed, as well as institution-building activities, a democratic control of political life and a fight against corruption and organised crime). Although the Mission tried to engage in such activities in co-operation with the OHR and the UN, this was done in an relatively *ad hoc* way, while the monitoring tasks remained the bulk of the work of the Mission's human rights branch.

We could thus wonder if the OSCE's role in the field of human rights in comprehensive peace-building operations, similar to the Bosnian one, would not be better adapted if it were focused on Rule of Law activities, such as the one mentioned above. One of the OSCE's institutions, the Office for Democratic Institutions and Human Rights (ODIHR), could furthermore contribute to developing a strategy and advise on implementing it since it has considerable expertise in that field.

Democratisation

The situation regarding democratisation follows from what has just been said about elections and human rights: Bosnia is not yet a democratic State. However, this is maybe one of the fields in which there has been much improvement. Democratisation tasks were initially not included in the Dayton Agreement, but it was realised in 1996 that the holding of democratic elections depended on the respect for basic political rights. Democratisation activities were thus added to those undertaken by the OSCE Human Rights Branch in order to improve the situation in that field. Because of a lack of time and because of the *ad hoc* nature of this adaptation, not much was achieved for the 1996 elections. In 1997, however, a separate branch was created within the Mission, which contributed to a relative improvement of the political climate in 1997 and again in 1998.

Although some activities were – and still are – focused on political party support, a lot was also done in the field of 'society democratisation'. This means that many activities were aiming at reconciliation, civil society development, or even addressed psycho-social issues. At the same time, other stated goals of the branch were the development of a rule of law, good governance and human rights dissemination. These activities are certainly valuable ones, but the question remains whether there are not simply too many of them, the subsequent risk being a dilution of the final impact of the branch. There is also a lack of clarification between the respective roles of the human rights branch and the democratisation one. Furthermore, I wonder whether gender issues, youth support activities and grass-roots projects, which are in fashion nowadays, would not be better left to NGOs, which have a significant expertise in such topics.

In fact, I would suggest that the OSCE, as a political international organisation, limits its democratisation strategy to developing a 'political democracy' and to focusing on improving the political life of the country so that free and fair elections are held. That would mean specialising in activities such as political party development and support (which the Mission is already doing with success), development of free media, training of national electoral staff, training of political candidates in good governance and training of NGOs specialised in electoral observation. This would already represent quite a lot of work for the twenty-nine democratisation officers disseminated on the territory of Bosnia and Herzegovina.

Conclusion

As a conclusion, I would like to underline that in situations such as the Bosnian one, where the whole political system has been destroyed and has to be recreated, the action of the OSCE and its fellow international organisations might be more efficient if aimed at reforming the society from the top down. One of the major challenges facing the international community in Bosnia today is to address the issue of over-powerful political parties controlling every aspects of the country's economic, social, legal and political life. One suggestion to try to fight this cancer would be to start with implementing the rule of law (OSCE's human rights branch) and holding free and fair elections in order to encourage the election of a democratic government (democratisation and election branches). This in itself requires a lot of time, money and human resources, but might prove more suitable and quicker than starting from the bottom (society democratisation) and working up. At the same time, NGOs (both international and local) could focus on democratising the society in depth through grass-roots projects and community development programmes. A better division of labour and establishment of priorities might then prove beneficial to the country, albeit carrying the risk of the international community appearing too intrusive. In order to avoid such a situation, this approach should follow the pattern of 'ownership' as developed by the High Representative, that is a progressive transfer of responsibility to the local actors, while making them more accountable to their co-nationals for their actions.

Chapter 5

Albania: Status Report

Geert-Hinrich Ahrens

In this chapter I report on the activities of the OSCE Presence in Albania. I have been asked to give an overview of the Mission, an assessment of its evolution to the present day, my views on the direction it will take in the future, and its place generally in the scheme of things when compared with developments in the region as a whole. I hope you will forgive me if I am a little selective in covering the subjects.

To give an overview of the Mission, I should start by explaining that it came into being as a response to the breakdown of law and order throughout Albania at the beginning of 1997. On the basis of emergency reports by the Personal Representative of the OSCE Chairman-in-Office, Dr Franz Vranitzky, the Permanent Council established, on 27 March 1997, an OSCE Presence in Albania. It was created in order to provide a flexible co-ordinating framework within which concerned international organisations could play their part in their respective areas of competence – all this as part of a coherent stabilisation strategy. In addition, the Permanent Council specifically directed the OSCE (in co-operation, *inter alia*, with the Council of Europe) to advise the Albanian authorities, and assist them with democratisation, the development of free media, the promotion of respect for human rights and the preparation and monitoring of the June/July 1997 elections.

Although Communism in Albania ended in 1991, many would draw a line in the sand in 1997, considering that Albania's path to democracy started from the beginning again after these elections. Certainly so much of the infrastructure had been destroyed that it was a very different setting under which the Socialist Party took power. From these early days, the Presence has expanded considerably in order to fully meet its remit to serve as this 'flexible co-ordinating framework', in concert of course with the Albanian Government. The established strength of the Presence staff in Albania is currently 120, although it is not at present fully manned. Of these posts, 55 are international, 65 are national, and roughly two-thirds are located at the Presence's seven field offices outside Tirana. The latter are an invaluable OSCE asset, giving the Organisation a degree of coverage, outreach and genuine 'presence' in the country, which is unique among international and diplomatic missions in Albania.

This expansion has essentially come about in reaction to the rapidly changing scene, as the country and its needs have developed and changed over these past two and a half years. It is often said that a week in politics is a long time in

Albania, and the Presence has lived through and had to adapt to many different situations in the relatively short time since its creation.

I can distinguish five distinct phases that have dictated the direction the Presence has taken. First, in those very early days there was a need for much political brokerage and mediation to enable the first post-crisis elections to take place. Second, this was followed by much election-orientated work to ensure that they duly took place in June and July of 1997. Third, once elections were over, the Presence was able to set about assisting with the establishment of its longer-term activities to consolidate democracy and the rule of law. A particular focus of the Presence work during this period was the organisation and holding of the referendum at the end of 1998, which approved the country's present Constitution. This focus on democratic consolidation and institution-building was interrupted by the Kosovo crisis, leading to a fourth distinct phase, with the need to substantially alter the role of the Presence to assist with the handling of the refugee influx that followed. The fifth phase sees us back to our longer-term activities, in support of what is now the third new Socialist Party Government since those elections of 1997.

To turn to our tasks in more detail, this 'flexible framework' I mentioned earlier has now developed, following the riots of September 1998, into the 'Friends of Albania' Group. Here, together with the European Union at international level, the Group brings together, in an informal forum, those countries and international organisations that are active in providing Albania with financial support, technical assistance and other forms of aid. It is essentially a means by which all the international partners, including both bilateral donors and major multilateral donors, along with the Government, can meet together to discuss the progress of reform, to call for action when necessary, and co-ordinate the assistance efforts to the country. Particular areas of priority are law and order and anti-corruption, both problems that the 'Friends' have lent support to and called upon the Government to tackle vigorously. Neither will be solved quickly, but the recent passing of a new State Police Law and a new Civil Service Law are examples of ways in which the building blocks of basic legislation have been put in place and are now there to be built upon. I should add that both laws received considerable input from the Presence's experts, as well as from other legal bodies, including of course the Council of Europe.

Other direct assistance is given to the Government by dedicated officers from the Presence. One works together with the Secretary-General of the Prime Minister. Another works with the Ministry of Economic Development and Trade, and members of the local 'Friends of Albania' Group, acting as a means to co-ordinate donor assistance. A third works with the Ministry of Local Government, and is heavily involved in both the pressing issue of decentralisation – this in itself a major challenge facing the country – as well as playing a major role in preparing for local elections next year. In this latter role, our liaison officer acts as co-ordinator for a number of donor agencies who have pledged support and assistance to the process. A new electoral law is needed, as are accurate voter's lists. There is much to do between now and the local elections next year.

Political mediation is an area where the Presence has had to take a leading role, particularly during last year. A fragile government and a highly polarised political scene made for a tense period, during which the Presence none the less contributed significantly to the difficult process of constitutional reform. For much of 1998 and indeed until September 1999, the opposition Democratic Party boycotted the Parliament and used street demonstrations as a means of protest. In September of last year violent street disturbances broke out in Tirana following the murder of a prominent DP activist, Azem Hajdari. The Presence played the leading role in mediating between what was left of the Government and the leaders of the opposition in restoring order and returning the offices of State institutions, many of which had been overrun by the rioters, to their rightful hands. Another, but far from exhaustive, area where this mediation role has been vital was in the solving of a hunger strike by judges, and the agreement to a formula by which they would be tested on their judicial knowledge. Another was the solving of a politically-motivated strike by students, all of who were demanding better conditions. This led to the first meeting of government and opposition party leaders, and was widely seen as the first easing of tension between the two sides. This search for compromise and the promotion of dialogue between opposing parties remains a high priority for the Presence, whether at national level or in handling the many local disputes which our field offices are frequently asked to mediate.

But there is much else that the Presence undertakes under its essentially 'democracy-building' mantle. There is a Legal Counsellor's Office, set up to encourage and promote the Rule of Law. Working in close co-operation with the ODIHR and the Council of Europe, the LCO, among much else, provides advice on legislation as it works through the legislative process, and this includes careful analysis to ensure that any new laws do not conflict with the new Constitution. I should add that last year a department of the LCO was also responsible for all technical aspects of this new Constitution, and is still involved in a civic education programme to promote greater awareness of it. A part of this office includes a Human Rights Alert Programme that monitors alleged violations, often involving cases resulting from the Communist era, and brings them to the attention of respective agencies, and the State.

This task of assisting in the development of both the democratic institutions of the State and the foundations of a civic society is followed up in other areas, the promotion of NGOs being particularly important. All NGOs in the country are very much in their infancy, and programmes, seminars and project-writing skills are but some of the areas that have been covered by a dedicated cell in the Presence. For next year there are ambitious plans to set up a nationwide network of regional NGO Resource Centres to further promote their work and build their capacities. Awareness-building in the area of women's rights and the encouragement of NGO activity in this area is another particular focus of the Presence's civic society-building work.

Another area is that of parliamentary observation. Here the observation of parliamentary practice and procedure has been undertaken by the Presence in the interests of promoting pluralism and the norms of civilised parliamentary behaviour. The results of this observation effort are presented in the form of reports circulated on a periodic basis to the Albanian Parliament itself, OSCE participating States, the Parliamentary Assemblies of the OSCE, Council of Europe and the European Parliament.

The environment also has a section devoted to it within the Presence, and in this field there is a huge amount to be done. It is a priority area and, working with both the Government and NGOs, I intend to bring much greater attention to the problems by promoting public awareness and a more developed sense of collective responsibility.

A press and public information section is involved both with the promotion of a free and democratic media, as well as being the mouthpiece for the Presence in its many and various activities.

Finally, in describing the work of the Presence, I should not leave out the part it played during the Kosovo crisis. Faced with the rapidly deteriorating situation in this neighbouring region in early 1998, it was decided that the Presence should take on a border-monitoring role. Accordingly a number of border-monitoring field offices were opened close to Albania's northern and eastern borders from March 1998 onwards. The reports of these monitors, somewhat 'unsung heroes', kept the international community informed of the deteriorating humanitarian and security situation before and during the fighting. Living as they did in difficult and dangerous circumstances, they worked through the escalation of the crisis when the first wave of some 25,000 refugees came to Albania in the summer of 1998 to escape the fighting, through to the international settlement this year. In addition, the whole Presence became involved during the period of March until mid-June this year, when Albania became the place of refuge for close to 500,000 Kosovo refugees, or almost 15 per cent of its native population. Here the Presence was able to greatly assist in establishing procedures and an operational plan to handle the refugee influx. It did so by giving its support, advice and loaning personnel for the setting up of an Emergency Management Group within the Prime Minister's Office, in order to assist and facilitate national and international relief efforts. In addition, the Presence was very active in supporting the effort on the ground by using all its field office assets, reinforced by ex-members of the Kosovo Verification Mission, to assist with handling the situation on the ground. Indeed in Bajram Curri, the field office located there was solely responsible for the managing of some 3,000 refugees; so remote and difficult was the situation at the time.

Let me now turn to my views on where the Presence stands in comparison to other missions in the Balkans. I must start by saying that there are very many differences between Albania and the countries and regions of the former Yugoslavia, where the majority of these missions are situated. The most obvious difference is that Albania never was a part of the former Yugoslavia, and therefore has never suffered directly from the tragic war that enveloped the Balkans during the early part of this decade. But Tito was a relatively benign dictator, certainly when compared to Hoxha. Hoxha left behind the poorest country in Europe, with very little in the way of an infrastructure to support development, and respective governments have struggled to establish a State and to bring about any form of national unity or collective responsibility. At the same time, it must be said that Albania at least does not suffer from the same ethnic tensions that have beset other parts of the Balkans. There are no religious conflicts, and hardly any minority problems. Instead, Albania's problems are, in the main, within Albania itself, borne of its own immaturity and vulnerability, and the fact that, despite its now nearly ten years of post-Communist rule, it still remains somewhat isolated from the European mainstream. This of course is no longer the result of deliberate policy, but simply because fragile Governments, a weak infrastructure, corruption and a tenuous security situation have prevented its becoming an attractive place for businessmen to invest in, or for visitors from the world at large to discover, despite its tremendous natural beauty and tourist potential.

It must, though, be said that however different Albania may be in terms of its present stage of development and recent history, many of the problems that currently beset it, whether in the area of organised crime, corruption or the difficulty of creating a professional and depoliticised public administration, also afflict the region as a whole, or large parts of it, and a more co-ordinated approach is needed to address them. Here the Presence, as a part of the wider Regional Strategy that the OSCE is pursuing in conjunction with the Stability Pact for South-Eastern Europe, believes it also has an important role to play.

It is against a background of needing to improve co-ordination and to address the problems of the region as a whole in a more comprehensive manner, that the OSCE Chairman-in-Office recently called for the development of a Regional Strategy within the OSCE. This Regional Strategy seeks, on the one hand, to contribute to the underlying aims of the Stability Pact for South-Eastern Europe by providing it with a more coherent OSCE approach to addressing the problems of the region. In effect, it is a framework for co-ordination with other international and regional operators, and, above all, for imparting the benefit of the OSCE's presence and experience on the ground. On the other hand, it represents a more systematic approach, by the OSCE itself, to the way the Organisation, and its missions themselves, work together in the region. As regards the latter, the Strategy aims to improve co-ordination among OSCE operations in the region, particularly in those areas where one mission has experience that may be useful to other missions. Or, where the underlying causes of instability transcend boundaries, and the OSCE can thus achieve more through this co-ordinated approach. The Stability Pact and the OSCE's regional approach are together an attempt by the international community to overcome the defects of its previous somewhat *ad hoc* approach to the region, promoting closer co-operation between its constituent States and peoples, and encouraging them to learn from one another's experiences in the difficult process of democratic transition in which they are all involved. The Presence in Albania very much welcomes this new development in the international approach to the region, and we are actively involved with our partner missions in exploring ways in which it can be exploited to the benefit of our Albanian hosts.

For the time being, therefore, the Presence is intensely involved, through its own efforts and working closely with partner missions and other international players, in trying to assist the process of Albania's integration in the Euro-Atlantic mainstream – which is where its Government and people rightly see their future. The Presence is for the moment a popular and respected mission, not always the case in all such missions deployed in the Balkans and elsewhere, and I hope that it will remain so. I believe that for the foreseeable future the Presence has a number of roles to fill.

First, it must continue to support the democratically elected Government, and encourage it to push through with its programmes, particularly in the areas of law and order and anti-corruption, giving assistance whenever called for. This assistance, we must also recognise, cannot only be in the area of institution-building and legislation, but must increasingly focus on the need to develop human capacities and resources to match. It is little use having high-quality democratic legislation on the Statute Book if the capacity is not there to implement the legislation properly. Capacity-building should therefore be an increasing focus of the activities of our missions and of the international donor community with whom we work.

Second, the Presence must also continue to work within its wide mandate in the main areas of decentralisation, NGO development, human rights, the environment and electoral reform. What I have just stated about capacity-building in the institutional area applies as much if not more to our work to encourage the growth of civic society.

Third, I believe that the Presence should continue to mediate where it can between Government and opposition, as well as to support the younger generation of politicians now emerging, who, untainted by the past, are more open than their predecessors to dialogue across party and ideological lines. It is clear to me that the current climate remains unduly influenced by the old guard political elite, for whom politics is more to do with power than with policies. Albania can no longer afford the luxury of this brand of politics, when so many of the problems facing it require national rather than party-political solutions.

Fourth, progress and development in the country is made more difficult by the poor reputation and image it suffers from abroad. Still not properly formed is the political will of the political class as a whole, whether in Government or opposition, to really address the problems of the people, which lie at the heart of criminality and corruption. Here I am talking about grass roots issues such as poverty, unemployment, health and education. These are problems that the Albanians themselves must resolve, though they are ones that the international community must also be aware of and be prepared to assist with.

Albania's role in the Balkans is a crucial one. It needs stability, particularly so given the continuing ethnic and political tensions in the neighbouring regions of Kosovo, Montenegro and the former Yugoslav Republic of Macedonia where ethnic Albanians are found. Democracy in the country is still a fragile and developing commodity, and I firmly believe that the need for international attention and support will remain, and at the same time be welcomed by the majority of the people, whose one aim is to shake off the legacy left by previous regimes, and begin to live in harmony with their neighbours and as responsible members of the international community.

Chapter 6

Kosovo: Status Report

Dan Everts

As far as the international community is concerned, the crisis in Kosovo should first be seen as the result of a preventive diplomacy failure. Despite early attempts to tackle the problem between 1989 and 1992–93, international actors proved unable to prevent tensions from deteriorating into an armed conflict. However, following NATO forces entry in Kosovo in June 1999, a new interesting experience of international governance was developed on the basis of United Nations Security Council Resolution 1244. In that context, the United Nations Mission in Kosovo (UNMIK) has a huge task to perform in order to rebuild a totally destroyed territory – not only physically, but also institutionally, economically and politically.

The International Governmental Structure

Drawing on the lessons from the implementation of the Dayton Agreement in Bosnia and Herzegovina, an integrated international structure has been created, headed by the UN SRSG for Kosovo and made of four pillars (UNHCR, UN Civil Administration, OSCE and the EU). This system is characterised by co-operation and synergy in clearly demarcated areas of competence. Within UNMIK, the OSCE Mission is specifically in charge of democratisation and institution-building. This includes the setting up of a judicial system, training of a police force and local administrators, monitoring human rights, developing of a free and independent media, and preparing and executing elections in Kosovo.

The question has been raised whether this very intrusive international presence was not a new form of protectorate. Understood in its nineteenth-century meaning, this notion is often perceived in a pejorative way. Quite surprisingly, some of its advocates can indeed be found amongst the Kosovars themselves. They would favour the international community to temporarily take charge of the situation, until the violence and tensions lessen. However, such a solution is very difficult to apply given the lack of human and financial resources of the United Nations. It would also have given a too narrow and unforeseen interpretation of UN Security Council resolution 1244.

What is needed is to co-opt and bring the Kosovars into the administration of Kosovo. We have to share responsibility for the governance of this province with the Kosovars without challenging the basic understanding of resolution 1244 being 'substantial autonomy' for Kosovo. Co-administration will give new impetus to the efficient and effective rebuilding of Kosovo through unified efforts, that is, the dissolution of all parallel structures.

Civil–Military Relations

Civil–military relations are better and of a higher level than ever, especially compared to Bosnia. Regular and intense institutionalised exchanges ensure a daily co-operation between KFOR, the UNMIK pillars and civil agencies. Moreover, KFOR is actively pursuing a broad CIMIC agenda. KFOR clearly realises its potential in supporting civil society through their technical and logistical expertise. For instance, KFOR is currently involved in a 'winterisation' programme. Although such support is valuable for the other international organisations, the primary role of the multinational force remains to guarantee a secure environment for the whole population.

And here lies one of the major issues currently facing the international community: the level of violence remains very high, despite the 48,000 soldiers deployed on the territory. This apparently paradoxical situation results in fact from the limited law enforcement capacities of the international community, which fuels a climate of impunity and lawlessness and increases human rights violations. The imbalance is striking, between a massive military presence and an understaffed international police staff (only 1,850 out of 4,000 planned police officers have been deployed). As long as the international police force remains understaffed, 'complemented' by a deficient judicial system, it is very easy to get away with theft, murder and other crimes. Evidently, this has a negative and discomforting effect on the population. It has also a harmful effect on the standing of the international community; we tell them what has to be done, but are unable to enforce what has been recommended. Within the overall effort to redress this contradiction, the OSCE plays an important role through the development and support of the judiciary and the education and development of a Kosovar police force.

OSCE Activities

Within UNMIK, the OSCE Mission is in charge of democratising Kosovo and setting up a local self-administration. Whereas the UN manages the present, the OSCE prepares for the future: the former is in charge of an international police force, the latter trains the local police; the UN currently appoints judges, the OSCE trains future ones. Both organisations should thus be seen as complementary. Concerning the OSCE, five main fields of action may be distinguished.

Rule of Law

This aspect is of the utmost importance for Kosovo. The OSCE is, in close cooperation with pillar II, working to set up an effective and efficient judicial system. The OSCE selects and trains judges and prosecutors for service in the legal system. Also, the OSCE monitors and reports on trials and detentions in Kosovo. The establishment of a judicial system and ensuring respect for the rule of law is a process that will take time.

Human Rights

The results of an intensive study prepared by the OSCE on Human Rights violations will be published on 6 December 1999. This report is made of two parts, one dealing with violations committed before and during NATO intervention (December 1998 to June 1999) and the second one focusing on the following period, between June and October 1999. This report shows that the violence which occurred during those two periods is very different in nature: while massive and State-sponsored violations were committed against Kosovo Albanians before June 1999, the following months were characterised by a persisting high level of incidents and violent acts, committed against minorities and most often inspired by revenge.

Media

Much attention is paid by the international community to the creation of independent media. Such a proposition receives the full support of the population, who are eager to see the development of free media outside governmental control, offering alternative sources of information. An important project being currently designed is the establishment of a 'Kosovo BBC', with the support of Switzerland, Norway and the Netherlands. Also, the Media House will give the opportunity for a wide spectrum of print media and radio and TV stations to deploy their activities and guarantee a diversified media spectrum.

Police School

The Kosovo Police Service School develops and educates the future police officers of Kosovo. The School envisages educating around 3,500 police officers, putting them through six weeks of intense basic training after which the graduates continue with nineteen weeks of field training. The classes are mixed, ethnically as well as gender-wise. The first class of graduates was welcomed across Kosovo and the increasing number of minorities in the second class (especially an increase in Serbs) shows that multi-ethnicity is an achievable goal.

Elections

These are at the heart of a current debate: tremendous pressure is being exerted, by both local and international actors, to hold elections by March 2000. Although having early elections is not a problem in itself, there is an absolute necessity to avoid premature ones. Minimum conditions need to be fulfilled in order to develop a democratic climate: free media, political party pluralism and a non-violent environment. Moreover, Kosovo is currently lacking a proper voters' list. A registration period has thus to be organised: this is not an easy task, especially since the great majority of previous civil registers have been destroyed and since many citizens have lost or been deprived of their own identity documents. At least six months would be needed to fulfil such a task. Although the election law has almost been totally drafted, the registration issue is therefore the main reason why elections should be delayed until later in 2000.

Chapter 7

The Former Yugoslav Republic of Macedonia: Status Report

Carlo Ungaro

Starting as the CSCE Mission in September 1992, the Spillover Monitor Mission to Skopje is the oldest still existing Mission of the OSCE. It is the smallest of the five South-Eastern Europe Missions with currently eight international and six local staff members. As its name suggests, the Skopje Mission's primary task is monitoring and reporting.

With the major transformation of the OSCE as an organisation, new tasks were devoted to the Mission. Its very size places restrictions on the ability it has to administer large projects, but it does play the role of a catalyst for many projects and developments through its regular contacts both with local authorities on all levels, and the international community.

Before starting to describe the activities in detail it is important to have a view of the host country, the way the Mission was established and its mandate. The host country, the Former Yugoslav Republic of Macedonia is located geographically in the centre of the Balkans and is of crucial importance for the stability of the region. The country of 2 million multi-ethnic inhabitants gained its independence peacefully, after a referendum in September 1991. Threats of a spillover of the neighbouring conflicts in Croatia and Bosnia, the collapse of State authority in Albania and the Kosovo war have damaged its economy and hampered economic reconstruction. The Former Yugoslav Republic of Macedonia has only recently begun to have cordial relations with its neighbours (namely Albania, Bulgaria and Greece) and preserving its stability still requires time and international support. This very stability is also fundamental for the future development of neighbouring Kosovo, because of the importance of the country as a hinterland and transit-way for the UNMIK–KFOR operations.

The decision to establish the Mission was taken in the context of the European Community's efforts to extend its Monitoring Mission (ECMM) to countries bordering Serbia and Montenegro in order to avoid the spread of tensions to those territories. In the first years, the Mission was running as a joint OSCE–ECMM Mission under one roof. It is worth noting also that when the Mission was set up the Former Yugoslav Republic of Macedonia had only observer status in the OSCE. The country became a full participating State in October 1995. When the

Mission started in September 1992, no other international organisation and less than a handful of diplomatic representations had opened in the capital Skopje.

To understand the scope and limitations of operational activities, it is worth taking a look at the framework of the Mission described in article 1 of the mandate:

> shall be established to monitor developments along the borders of the Host country with Serbia in order to preserve territorial integrity; to promote the maintenance of peace, stability and security; and to prevent possible conflicts in the region. The monitor Mission shall therefore engage in talks with governmental authorities of the Host party and shall establish contacts with representatives of political parties and other organisations and with ordinary citizens. The Mission shall conduct trips to assess the level of stability as well as the possibility of conflict and unrest throughout the region. The Mission shall engage in such other activities as are compatible with the goals as stated in this Article. If conflicts should occur, the monitor Mission shall assist in establishing the facts in order to avoid further deterioration.

The formula for the external and internal stability of the country opens possibilities for activities in inter-ethnic relations, political, economic and social stability. The level of co-operation and understanding with the existing government was, and still is important.

Review of Operational Activities

As has already been stressed there was a specific situation in the first years of the Mission. Here was a State with enormous difficulties, with almost no diplomatic representations and crisis situations on two of four borders. It was isolated having lost the main transport roads to Western Europe, and ignored by the international media which were focusing on the wars in Croatia and Bosnia and Herzegovina. This specific situation, together with the mandate, formed the basis for the activities of the Mission, which in the early years were mainly preventive diplomacy functions: monitoring the borders, collecting information on the country and reporting to the OSCE organs, the Member States and the international community about developments.

Monitoring Operations

These monitoring operations of the border areas were carried out from 1993 to 1999 in close and excellent co-operation with the military units of the United Nations Preventive Deployment Force (UNPREDEP) deployed along the northern and western borders, UN military observers and UN police units. The UN activities were restricted to the border areas, while the Mission had its presence throughout the host country. The Mission's specific task was therefore to collate all information from both the border and the rest of the country to produce an overall political assessment.

With the slow but steady increase in the number of countries and international organisations, the Mission undertook an anchor function. It established and hosted a weekly international meeting as a forum for exchange of information on security- and stability-related subjects in order to define common positions. Even though there are now several more specific meetings of the EU, the World Bank, UNHCR and so on, the Mission's meeting continues to be a focal point for exchange of political information and activity reports with UNMIK, UNHCR, UNDP, ICRC, IFRC, ECMM, EC, KFOR and bilateral embassies.

Inter-Ethnic Relations: The Co-operation with the High Commissioner on National Minorities

For the internal stability of the country, the inter-ethnic relations, particularly those between the majority ethnic Macedonians and the (officially) 25 per cent ethnic Albanian population, were and continue to be of crucial importance. From the beginning, the Mission has followed closely the evolution of inter-ethnic relations. In a complex political environment it has tried, through its permanent presence and specific initiatives, to play a constructive and stabilising role in the country. To achieve this goal, the Mission is in permanent contact with all relevant political factions and opinion leaders, and has very close co-operation with the office of the High Commissioner on National Minorities (HCNM), Max van der Stoel. In 1995, it helped, with the support of the HCNM, to defuse ethnic tensions which had led to mass confrontations relating to the establishment of a private ethnic Albanian university in the west of the country in Tetovo – unsanctioned by the Government. The problem of university education in the minority Albanian language is still unresolved, although a compromise may be reached soon, thanks to the continuous and patient work of the HCNM. The question of inter-ethnic relations has always been important, but it is now becoming one of the priority tasks of the Mission. One Mission member is now working exclusively in this field and acting as liaison to the office of the HCNM.

In Co-operation with ODIHR: Election Monitoring

The host country has made remarkable progress in the development of democracy. The Mission contributed to ODIHR election monitoring through its intimate knowledge of the political scene and its full manpower resources during the monitoring of the local elections in 1996, the parliamentary elections in 1998 (which led to a peaceful change in government) and the presidential elections in 1999. The Mission founded a weekly political meeting before the 1998 parliamentary elections, with representatives of international political foundations, organisations and political officers of interested OSCE Member States embassies. Since then, that meeting has become an 'institution'.

Local Self-Government, Economy and Ecology

Further new fields of interest for the Mission were the decentralisation of the State and the economic and social dimension of security and stability of the host country. The development of a functioning local self-government is a priority for the Mission in the move towards decentralisation and vitalisation of the economy. Visits to municipalities, discussions with the local authorities and the newly-created Ministry for Local Self-Government, as well as consultations with all relevant international organisations working in this field, are part of the regular activities of the Mission. An unemployment rate approaching 40 per cent and 150,000 families depending upon social care led the Mission to investigate and publish reports on the economic situation.

Before addressing the specific activities of the Mission and regional co-operation, let us briefly look at its role during the Kosovo crisis.

The Kosovo Crisis and the Following Months

After the first outbreak of violence in Kosovo in early 1998, the OSCE reacted by reinforcing the Mission, as well as its presence in Albania. Particular attention was paid to the mountainous and almost inaccessible border with Kosovo. After a relatively stable period, a dramatic escalation of violence led to a massive arrival of refugees at the northern Macedonian border. At the same time, the monitoring was made more difficult because of the end of the UNPREDEP mandate, following the Chinese veto in the Security Council. As a consequence, only eight members of the Spillover Monitor Mission and a similar number of ECMM staff remained in the field (instead of the 790 members of UNPREDEP), at least until the evacuated Kosovo Verification Mission (KVM) engaged in the monitoring.

The Mission, however, managed to fulfil its traditional task – to monitor the border – while getting an overview of the influx of refugees. It was on the spot during the dramatic increase of movements at the Blace border, when 60,000 refugees were stranded in a 'no-man's-land' muddy field. The Mission assumed responsibility for reporting, awareness-raising, and establishing contacts between humanitarian and governmental actors, in order to overcome communication problems and increase the level of co-operation. The arrival of 360,000 Kosovo-Albanian refugees (about 15 per cent of Macedonia's own population) also threatened inter-ethnic relations, thus representing the most serious challenge for the country since its independence. In co-operation with the HCNM, the Mission focused on early-warning activities. With ODIHR and UNHCR, it additionally ran training seminars for the border police and refugee camp police officers. Finally, Mission members raised the awareness of the international community on the negative impact of the crisis on the Macedonian economy.

Current Activities and New Tasks within the Framework of Regional Co-operation and the Stability Pact

Following the Kosovo crisis, many countries decided to allocate funds for bilateral aid and development projects in Macedonia. Most of them, however, lacked sufficient representation, as well as the necessary in-depth understanding of the country. In this regard, the Mission assumed the role of a project-catalyst and facilitator, providing briefing on requested topics or channelling proposals to various local actors (mayors, NGO's, villages and so on) through its broad contact network. The Mission also helped those groups by counselling them on how to formulate concrete projects and to whom they should be addressed.

In support of the reform programme of the Government, the Mission continues to focus on the Local Self-Government (LSG) project. A group of Mayors, representing the various political, ethnic and regional trends of the country, was established as a focus group to discuss and develop the formation of LSG. The Ministry of LSG co-operates in this project and will send a representative for the first study tour of the group to Bavaria in January 2000. The main objective is to demonstrate how a decentralised administration works, and to underline the regional economic development generated by Bavarian municipalities. It is also hoped that personal contacts established between the Mayors on that occasion will lead to further co-operation. Several OSCE member States have proposed to organise similar study tours, co-organised by the Mission. In the course of the year 2000, a joint trans-border project with the OSCE Presence in Albania working on LSG will start. Preparatory meetings have already been held to design appropriate projects – including a cross-border minority one. In such projects, where the Mission and the Presence will be able to use their grass-root knowledge of the local scene, both of them are interested in co-operating with the Council of Europe and other international organisations.

Security-related issues concerning the border area will also remain of primary importance for the Mission. A joint workshop for Mayors and border officials from municipalities on the western and northern borders is planned for the coming year, to encourage them to overcome their problems of co-operation. The Mission is also going to organise and moderate 'hearings' between the indigenous population and their local authorities (most of whom are ethnic Albanian) and the border units of the army and the police (predominantly ethnic Macedonians) in order to reduce tensions in sensitive border areas.

The major problems of trafficking throughout the country and the region are being addressed in collaboration with the Ministries of the Interior and of Defence and will continue to be treated with interest. ODIHR, supported by the Mission, will also continue to organise police training seminars in the coming year 2000. Another important field of co-operation with ODIHR will be the organisation of a seminar for young Roma leaders in Kumanovo in December 1999, aiming at establishing a European-wide association of young Roma leaders. The Mission will continue to support the activities of the HCNM on minority issues. Among these, education will receive much attention, especially directed at finding a compromise formula for higher education in the Albanian language.

In the context of the joint efforts of the five Missions constituting the South-Eastern Europe regional dimension, the Mission leads the important project of setting up a legislative or legal clearing house. This project has been received with great interest by all the Working Tables. The Mission is now addressing funding. For this project, as for most of the others, the Mission needs the co-operation of others since there is no funding in the limited budget for such purposes. The future engagement in other projects, within the framework of the South-Eastern Europe regional dimension of the OSCE, or within the framework of the tables and working groups of the Stability Pact, will depend also on the availability of sufficient funding.

The Spillover Monitor Mission remains ready and able to make its contribution to wider co-operation through its long-term experience of the region.

Chapter 8

The Operational Role of the OSCE in the Field of Conflict Prevention: An Assessment of the Spillover Monitor Mission to Skopje (Macedonia)

Emeric Rogier

The Spillover Monitor Mission to Skopje was established in September 1992 as a result of a mounting concern in the Western countries, and especially within the Bush administration, that the conflict in Bosnia and Herzegovina might spread to Macedonia and finally degenerate in a wider Balkan war, involving among others two NATO members (Greece and Turkey). However, Macedonia does not share any border with Bosnia. The very notion of 'spillover' seems thus disputable in this context. It reflects the fact that the Yugoslav conflict was essentially considered a civil war and more generally that its dynamics were misunderstood. Still, the viability of the newly independent Macedonia was endangered by both external and internal threats. The OSCE presence was consequently willingly accepted by President Gligorov at a time when Macedonia suffered from isolation and a lack of recognition from both Western countries and international bodies. Paradoxically, the country was not granted full membership in the OSCE until 1995, as 'the Former Yugoslav Republic of Macedonia'. This is another contradiction since the best way to support this State would have been to recognise it as such, instead of waiting for so many years and giving it a kind of nickname.

Review of Activities

If preventive diplomacy relates to the setting up of a process of peaceful change, then the OSCE Mission in Macedonia has not been really engaged in preventive diplomacy. In fact, it served as a political antenna, it performed early-warning functions, but it was not involved in direct mediation activities, neither between the Macedonian authorities and their neighbours, nor between the Macedonian Government and the representatives of the Albanian minority.

For instance, the Mission monitored the border with Serbia and was thus in a position to inform the OSCE headquarters in Vienna of Serbian incursions and other incidents, but it did not take part in the negotiations about the demarcation of the border. The Mission raised awareness of the consequences of the Greek embargo, but did nothing to find a solution to the dispute between the two countries – which was negotiated by the UN Special Envoy Cyrus Vance. The Mission was in touch with Albanian and Bulgarian authorities and tried to increase confidence between them and the Macedonian authorities, but this was only done incidentally and it did not go very far.

The same remark applies to the role of the Mission regarding the internal situation. The stability of the country was seen as endangered by the tense relationship between the Albanian minority and the Slavo-Macedonian majority. It was assumed that this situation could only worsen in the context of economic deterioration and would further worsen if the Macedonian nationalist party came to power. However, the Mission did not help to set up a process of dialogue and negotiations between the representatives of the Albanian minority and the Government. It did formulate advice and try to promote restraint but only on specific occasions, when serious incidents occurred (for instance, the Tetovo affair in 1995 and the Gostivar events in 1997). Generally speaking, the role of the Mission was to provide information, briefings and logistical support to others, especially to the High Commissioner on National Minorities (HCNM). How to explain this rather restricted role of the OSCE Mission? Three reasons may be put forward.

A Limited Mandate

Compared to other preventive missions in the Baltic States or in the Ukraine, the mandate of the OSCE Mission to Macedonia is much more restricted and somewhat less intrusive. The Mission has been deployed to 'monitor developments ... in order to promote the maintenance of peace, stability and security and to help prevent a possible conflict'. According to the Memorandum of Understanding concluded with the host country, it is tasked to engage in talks, establish contacts, conduct assessment trips and establish the facts when necessary. It is, however, doubtful that the monitoring of a situation is enough in itself to prevent the worsening of it. The discrepancy between the broad and fairly vague goals given to the Mission (to promote peace) and the tasks it is entitled to fulfil (in a word, fact-finding) is striking.

In a sense, these tasks were almost contradictory to 'real' preventive diplomacy. At the beginning, the Mission was deployed to underline the attention granted to this country by the 'international community' and as such, it was supposed to adopt a high profile. However, such a high profile not only appeared not enough to deter an external aggression – that is the reason why the United Nations later deployed a preventive military force on the border with Serbia – but it actually seems inadequate for the solving of internal tensions. As the experience of the HCNM shows, confidentiality and a low profile are required when dealing with minority issues. Thus, it was not always easy for the Mission to reconcile different priorities. By the same token, reporting and mediating are not easily reconciled: how to engage in preventive diplomacy and gain the confidence of the parties if the mediator is supposed to inform on a bi-weekly basis more than fifty States on the progress of the negotiations?

Too Many Cooks

In any case, the field of mediation was assumed by other people or bodies. Among them were the Working Group on Ethnic and National Communities and Minorities of the International Conference on Former Yugoslavia, the High Commissioner on National Minorities and the Civil Branch of the UN Preventive Deployment Force. To these mediators can be added numerous NGOs, diplomatic missions and rapporteur missions sent by the Council of Europe and other international organisations. That definitely makes too many people trying to improve the so-called 'inter-ethnic relations' – 'too many cooks' as the former Head of Mission, Ambassador Anderson, put it.[1] This situation raises obvious difficulties. On the one hand, it was maybe wiser for the OSCE Mission to refrain from getting itself involved in mediation. But on the other, its activities can not be considered as truly preventive.

This might have been a missed opportunity: had the Mission been provided with a stronger mandate, it could then have supported the Government and its quest for recognition and protection in exchange for a commitment to engage in reforms and improve the situation of the Albanian minority. In other words, if the Mission had been given the sole or at least the main responsibility of preventive diplomacy in this country, it could have had more leverage on the parties. Instead of this, none of the different mediators was in a position to provide firm inducements towards the Macedonian authorities (and the Albanian representatives as well) and the Mission actually supported the Gligorov administration without preconditions.

The Dependence on the Macedonian Authorities

Here lies the third reason that may explain the limited role and impact of the OSCE Mission in Macedonia. The Mission did not really lack impartiality, nor was its judgement biased in favour of the Government. But it avoided to being too critical, fearing this could weaken the Gligorov administration. For instance, the Mission has almost never mentioned human rights violations committed by the Macedonian police. If this attitude is understandable in the short run, it seems problematic in the longer run. It stems from the fact that right from the beginning, President Gligorov and his Government have been considered as the best chance for peace in the

---

[1] Cf. Norman Anderson, 'OSCE Preventive Diplomacy in the former Yugoslav Republic of Macedonia', *Helsinki Monitor*, 10:2 (1999), pp. 57–58.

country and as a stability factor in the region. It is true that the Macedonian regime has not behaved in an aggressive manner, neither towards its neighbours nor its population. But it has not improved substantially the situation of the country either. In Macedonia, being moderate does not necessarily mean being reformist – in the economic sphere as well as regarding minority issues. Thus, if the Gligorov administration was committed to dialogue, it appeared reluctant to address Albanian grievances, considering moreover that the Albanian activism was imported from outside, namely from extremists in Kosovo. For sure, the so-called moderates were under pressure from more radical elements and this was not an easy situation. To be fair to the OSCE Mission it should be mentioned that this cautious approach was also followed by many participating States.

Generally speaking, the role of the 'international community' in Macedonia is more controversial than it appears. Some observers consider that too much attention has been given to the Albanian minority, to the neglect of other minorities and of course the Slavo-macedonian majority. These detractors would then argue that the international involvement in this country had the perverse effect of escalating the situation. This may well be true too and has to be related to the number of mediators involved. On the one hand, internal tensions in Macedonia were internationalised and some elements tried to exploit this situation. On the other hand, the priority given to the 'stability' of the country did not prompt the authorities to engage in reforms. Finally, not only did the situation of the Albanian minority not improve substantially, but the so-called radicals (from both the Albanian and the Macedonian sides) came to power.

Conclusions

The OSCE Mission was not useless, but underused. It acted as an information agency instead of the lead agency it could have been with another mandate.[2] To put things provocatively, the OSCE Mission to Skopje was useful to the OSCE, to Skopje (meaning the Government) and only afterwards to Macedonia itself.

Macedonia survived the Kosovo conflict thanks to the wisdom (to be confirmed) of the newly elected Government and to the NATO bombings, which while not preventing the Albanians from being expelled at least allowed them to

---

[2] It may be noticed in this respect that the Mission comprised four monitors only between 1996 and 1998. After the Dayton Agreement was concluded in November 1995, discussions were engaged between the OSCE organs and the Macedonian authorities, the latter wishing the Mission to be transformed into a regional office seemingly to reduce the Organisation's intrusiveness – especially regarding 'inter-ethnic relations'. A sort of interim solution was found to maintain the Mission with its original mandate but with a reduced staff. Later on, events in the neighbourhood (crises in Albania and then in Kosovo) postponed the transformation of the Mission, which was then reinforced upon a decision from the Permanent Council of the OSCE (PC.DEC/218, 11 March 1998).

return quickly. This may well be the sole positive point of NATO's intervention. However, this tragic situation also occurred because the Western powers proved unable and unwilling to tackle the problem earlier.

Finally, the concept of 'stability', coined for instance in the Stability Pact for South Eastern Europe, sounds like a *faux-ami*. What is needed, and the Macedonia case illustrates this, is peaceful change. In this respect, the OSCE Mission should focus less on reporting and act more as an intermediary between the donors (that is, the European Union) and the Government. As such it could promote, and help finance, a peaceful change of the Macedonian situation, taking into account the recommendations of the HCNM. At the same time, there is a need to rationalise and probably to reduce the international presence in this country. Otherwise, the focus on 'inter-ethnic relations' and 'inter-ethnic conflict' might appear like a self-fulfilling prophecy.

PART II
THE DEVELOPMENT OF REGIONAL STABILITY IN SOUTH-EASTERN EUROPE

Chapter 9

The OSCE and the Stability Pact for South-Eastern Europe

Victor-Yves Ghebali

The end of military operations undertaken by NATO against the Federal Republic of Yugoslavia (FRY) coincided day-for-day with the launch on 10 June 1999 of a multilateral process aimed at the long-term consolidation of the Balkan region: the Stability Pact for South-Eastern Europe. The idea for such an enterprise was proposed by Germany during the Kosovo war and immediately endorsed by the European Union. Drafted at Petersberg by the political directors and senior officials of the European Union on 26 and 27 May 1999, the Pact was adopted by the Ministers for Foreign Affairs on 10 June. The approval of the objectives and principles of the Pact took place on 29 and 30 July 1999 during a summit at Sarajevo bringing together, under the European Union presidency, thirty or so Heads of State or Government and heads of a large number of international organisations. The operational phase of the process started with the decisions taken at Brussels by the South-Eastern Europe Regional Table at its inaugural meeting on 16 September 1999.[1] As the only security organisation then operationally active in five key countries of the region, the OSCE was requested to make a particularly significant contribution to the process initiated through the Stability Pact. Accordingly, as early as 1 July 1999, it decided to place the latter under its 'auspices', that is to say to work for compliance with the provisions of the Pact in accordance with its procedure and established principles. As a direct consequence of that decision, the OSCE also adopted, in March 2000, a Regional Strategy for South-Eastern Europe in support of the Stability Pact. The aim of the present paper is to present the main thrust of the Stability Pact (from the perspective of its actors, objectives and structures), assess the first steps towards its implementation and analyse its impact on the OSCE.

---

[1] For the Cologne Declaration, Sarajevo Declaration and other statements, see Stability Pact: *Official Text* published by the Office of the Special Co-ordinator (58pp).

The Actors of the Stability Pact

The Stability Pact constitutes an original process whose key actors are States and international institutions working in constant interplay.

State actors include, firstly, those countries who are to be the direct beneficiaries of the Pact: Albania, all the successors to the Former Yugoslavia (except for the FRY) as well as other States like Bulgaria, Hungary, Romania and Turkey. The sidelining of the FRY was supposed to be only provisional, depending on Serbia's democratisation.[2] However, the FRY is *de facto* involved in certain activities (those related to the return of refugees and displaced persons) due to its initial membership, since 1992, to an associated organ of the Pact: the Working Group on Humanitarian Issues, managed by the United Nations High Commissioner for Refugees. Furthermore Montenegro has been authorised to participate in all the activities of the Pact in full respect of the FRY's sovereignty and territorial integrity.[3]

The beneficiary countries are not expected to passively receive aid. In accordance with the Cologne Declaration, they have undertaken to achieve domestic economic and democratic reforms and also to co-operate among themselves bilaterally and regionally with the aim of promoting their individual integration within the Euro-Atlantic economic and security structures. In return, all the other actors of the Pact (States and international institutions) have pledged to help the countries concerned to accomplish rapid and measurable progress in this direction.[4] In other words, the Stability Pact is considered to be the 'ownership' of the countries of the region – which means that the final success or failure of the Pact rests on the will and concrete acts of those States.

The category of State actors also includes external contributors, that is to say the countries disposed to supply an economic and/or a political contribution to the process of stabilisation of South-Eastern Europe: the European Union countries, the extra-European members of the G-8 (the United States, Russia, Canada, Japan) as well as a number of other interested countries such as Switzerland; the Stability Pact was thus conceived in a pan-European perspective comparable both to that of the OSCE and the European Bank for Reconstruction and Development (EBRD). Although the Cologne Declaration refers to 'Participating' countries and 'Facilitating' countries (the second term apparently referring to Canada and Japan), this formal distinction however has no practical significance: all the actors

---

[2] The Cologne Declaration (second section of paragraph 11) states that the FRY will only become a full member of the process after the political settlement of the Kosovo crisis on the basis of principles adopted by the ministers of the G8 and with due consideration for the necessity for all the countries of the Pact to be in a position to respect its principles and objectives – which include democracy and the rule of law. Yugoslavia was eventually accepted as a formal and full participant in October 2000.

[3] See the third section of paragraph 11 of the Cologne Declaration and paragraph 4 of the Sarajevo Declaration.

[4] Paragraph 8 of the Cologne Declaration.

in the process can and do participate on an equal footing in the structures and activities of the Pact.

As to the category of institutional actors, it is remarkably wide and diversified. Indeed, the Pact involves the active contribution of a multitude of security, economic or financial institutions of universal, transregional or regional type (the UN, UNHCR, IMF, World Bank, OCDE, OSCE, NATO, WEU, European Commission, the Council of Europe, EIB, EBRD, UN/ECE), as well as sub-regional structures or 'regional initiatives' such as the Royaumont Process, the Organisation of the Black Sea Economic Co-operation, the Central European Initiative, the South-East Co-operation Initiativeand so on.[5] The basic texts of the Pact formally refer to 'participating' institutions (the European Union, the OSCE and the Council of Europe) and 'facilitating' institutions (all the others); here again the distinction has no practical significance.

The Objectives of the Stability Pact

The Stability Pact has been conceived to encourage the development of politically democratic regimes in South-Eastern Europe; prosperous market economies, as well as peaceful, open and pluralistic societies. Accordingly, it includes three interrelated fundamental objectives: democratisation, economic prosperity and sustainable peace.

The first objective focuses on the democratisation of a region where democracy has never blossomed. This means the encouragement of free and fair elections, the effective respect for human rights, the independence and freedom of the media, the accountability of legislative organs to their constituents, the independence of the judiciary, the fight against corruption, the deepening and strengthening of civil society, the protection of national minorities and the safe return of refugees and displaced persons to their homes.

As to the objective of economic prosperity, it encompasses reconstruction of devastated or ailing economies, fostering economic co-operation in the region and between the region and the rest of Europe and the world, the integration of the concerned countries into the world trade system and so forth. All this involves *inter alia* the suppression of political and administrative obstacles to the free circulation of goods and capital, the improvement of basic regional infrastructures and the fight against corruption and organised crime.

The third objective, which relates to the establishment of a lasting peace between the states and the peoples of the region, targets such specific goals as the fight against terrorism, crisis prevention, the elaboration and implementation of arms control agreements and CSBMs, the effective control of armed forces by democratic civilian authority, the control of arms trading, the reduction of military expenditure and armed forces and so forth.

---

[5] Paragraphs 33–38 of the Cologne Declaration.

In a nutshell, the three sets of objectives largely correspond to the three OSCE 'dimensions'. In fact the Stability Pact can be seen as a sort of operational 'Balkan Helsinki'.

The Structures of the Stability Pact

Conceived in a spirit of extreme pragmatism and motivated by the basic concern of avoiding overlapping and bureaucracy, the structures of the process are few and light. They consist of three elements:

- A South-Eastern Europe Regional Table meeting (without a fixed timetable) alternatively at Brussels and Thessaloniki. Open to all the Pact's States and intergovernmental actors, it is the policy-making organ of the process which issues directives pertaining to procedure and to concrete matters to the organs of the Pact. Its main task is to co-ordinate the activities of the subordinate organs and to evaluate the progress accomplished by the process.
- Three Working Tables (Democratisation and Human Rights; Economic Reconstruction, Development and Co-operation; Security Issues). Equally open without discrimination to all the process's actors, these tables are in fact specialised working groups whose task is to examine a given set of problems and to identify the necessary means of response. The Working Tables can sit by rotation in the countries of the region or elsewhere, for example at Vienna with an OSCE invitation. The regularity of their meetings is not fixed, but depends on purely practical necessities. The place and the time of work should where possible be determined so as to allow the participants to attend more than one table at a time –the most important aspect being that each Table remains free to develop its own dynamic.
- A Special Co-ordinator, appointed by the European Union after consultation with the OSCE Chairman-in-Office, chairs the Regional Table. He submits periodic reports to the Chairman-in-Office of the OSCE in the name of the Regional Table. The post is currently filled by Mr. Bodo Hombach (Germany),[6] who has a small secretariat (around 20 people) established at Brussels.

---

[6] M. Hombach was designated to this post in June 1999 by the Heads of State and of Government of the European Union meeting at Rio on the sidelines of the Europe/Latin America and Caribbean Summit (see *Atlantic News*, 3121 [30 June 1999], p. 1). See also paragraph 12 of the Sarajevo Declaration.

The First Implementation Steps of the Stability Pact

Meeting in Brussels on 16 September 1999 the Round Table for South-Eastern Europe adopted a number of practical arrangements on the basis of which the Working Tables started to function the following month.[7]

Initially chaired by the OSCE's High Commissioner on National Minorities (HCNM) and co-chaired by Hungary (until 30 June 2000), the Working Table on Democratisation and Human Rights held its first meeting at Geneva on 18 and 19 October 1999. It decided to concentrate on seven main themes or issues, each being assigned to the direction of an international institution or to a State in concert with one or several international organisations:[8]

Issues	Co-ordinator(s)
Human rights and national minorities	Slovenia, Council of Europe, HCNM
Good governance	Council of Europe
Media	United Kingdom
Gender issues	OSCE
Return of refugees and displaced persons	HCR
Co-operation on education	Austria, 'Reinforced Graz Process'
Inter-parliamentary co-operation	Royaumont Process

For each of the first of the four above-mentioned subjects the Working Table considered it necessary to set up a special task force charged with drawing up a list of existing programmes, identifying possible complementarity, formulating priorities and selecting the projects to instigate.

Attributed to Slovenia, the Council of Europe and the HCNM of the OSCE, the Human Rights and National Minorities Task Force has been mandated to elaborate an action plan to eliminate ethnic tensions in the region; this programme has been presented during a conference held in Portoroz (Slovenia) on 16–17 March 2000.[9] At the same time, it has been called to focus on the problems of a specific ethnic minority whose situation is constantly deteriorating since the end of the Cold War: the Roma and Sinti (Gypsies).[10] The goal here is to elaborate at a regional level concrete measures of protection in favour of this legitimate component of the societies and cultures of the countries of South-Eastern Europe. It is expected that

---

[7] The decisions taken by the Round Table are in *Official Texts*, op. cit., pp. 24–43.
[8] See *Official Texts*, pp. 44–48.
[9] See OSCE document PC/DEL/99/00 of 24 February 2000.
[10] The populations known by the generally pejorative term 'Gypsy' total between 9 and 12 million in the world, of which about 6 to 10 million are in Europe – notably in Romania (2.2 million) and Bulgaria (more than 600,000) and in the countries of the Former Yugoslavia. They form three groups: the Roma (Central and Eastern Europe), the Sinti (Germany, Italy, France) and the Kalé (Spain, Portugal and France). The Roma represent alone 90 per cent of the three groups.

this will boost the activities of the Warsaw-based 'Contact Point' for questions relative to Roma and Sinti run by the OSCE in co-operation with interested Governments, inter-governmental organisations (particularly the Council of Europe) and NGOs since 1995.[11]

As to the Good Governance Task Force entrusted to the Council of Europe, it aims to help the countries of the region create institutions for the protection of human rights and of national minorities (particularly ombudsman-type institutions) and to link them into a network at a regional level in order to fight against corruption, as well as to promote an increase in the efficiency of local administrations and trans-frontier co-operation. In this regard, Hungary organised at Szeged on 7 and 8 October 1999 a conference bringing together the Mayors of municipalities run by members of the Serb opposition, representatives of the Yugoslav free media and Mayors of European cities to debate on the role of local administration, democratic use of the media, and the economic and humanitarian assistance to supply to anti-Milosevic municipalities – an event which ended up in the setting up by the City of Szeged of a public fund to which the Hungarian Government at once decided to contribute up to 350 million forints.[12] It should also be noted that the question of good governance (which is closely related to the fight against corruption) has been included on the agendas of the three Working Tables of the Stability Pact.

Given the devastating role played by the media in the development of ethnic hatred, particularly during the Yugoslav conflicts, a task force placed under United Kingdom direction has been dedicated to the issue of free and independent media. Its mandate is to promote the freedom of expression in the whole region with particular emphasis in the FRY. One of its first concrete tasks is to elaborate on the basis of British proposals a Charter for South-Eastern Europe Media, providing *inter alia* for the abolition of State censorship, the political neutrality of journalists and the non-employment in the media of people subject to indictment by the International Criminal Tribunal for the Former Yugoslavia.[13] International organisations normally expected to make a major contribution to the task force are the Council of Europe and also the OSCE which disposes since 1998 of a particularly dynamic Representative on Freedom of the Media.[14]

The subject of gender issues has been attributed to the OSCE. This institution, which since 1998 pays increasing attention to the role of women in public life and

---

[11] Established within the Office for Democratic Institutions and Human Rights (ODIHR) of the OSCE, the Contact Point functions essentially as a centre for the collection and distribution of legislative and other information. For more details, see the recommendations formulated by the latest OSCE Review Meeting held in 1999 at Vienna and Istanbul (OSCE document RC.GAL/175/99, 19 November 1999, pp. 30–32).

[12] See OSCE document PC.DEL/527/99, 14 October 1997. See also *Official Texts*, p. 39.

[13] For the basic ideas which the United Kingdom proposed to include in the Charter, see *Official Texts*, p. 40.

[14] On this point see the 1998/99 *Yearbook* published by the OSCE Representative on the Freedom of the Media.

civil society, is to manage the activities of a specialised task force. Composed of a mix of governments and NGOs, the task force is charged with proposing an action plan in favour of gender equality including the field of political life.[15]

For the three remaining themes, the working table considered it preferable to use already existing mechanisms. The fundamental theme of the return of refugees and displaced persons was thus entrusted to the Working Group on Humanitarian Issues, managed by the United Nations High Commissioner for Refugees, firstly under the auspices of the International Conference on the Former Yugoslavia (1992–96) and then under the direction of the special organ following the implementation of the Dayton Agreement, namely the Peace Implementation Council.[16] Let us remember that the bloody conflicts which characterised the break-up of Yugoslavia provoked an exodus of more than 3 million people in the region of South-Eastern Europe. At the end of 1999, international action, led essentially by the UNHCR on the basis of the mandate formulated in Annex 7 of the Dayton Agreement, allowed the return of a million and a half refugees and displaced persons. But these partial returns have settled nothing; in most cases those repatriated live with little personal security, cannot find work and are not able to recover their properties. Considering the absence of a political environment respectful of human rights and offering basic economic security, the conditions for a lasting solution are obviously not in place.[17] The underlying causes of the massive exodus of people in the region continue because, as is well known, the ethnic cleansing was the objective and not just the consequence of the armed atrocities. The decision to integrate the Working Group on Humanitarian Issues into the Stability Pact process is all the more relevant as the Group includes the FRY as a full member.

The issue of co-operation on education and youth has been attributed to a recently-formed multilateral forum: the Graz Process. In November 1998 while Austria held the European Union Presidency it organised at Graz a conference of experts on the role of co-operation on educational matters for peace, stability and democratisation in South-Eastern Europe. The extension of this initiative led to the creation in December 1998 of a working organ (chaired and financed by the Austrians) known as the Graz Process. Encompassing the European Commission,

---

[15] For OSCE activities in this field, see *Annual Report of the Secretary General, 1 December 1997–30 November 1998* (OSCE document SEC.DOC/2/98, 2 December 1998, pp. 69–70).

[16] The Working Group on Humanitarian Issues was instituted in 1992 by the Geneva International Conference on the Former Yugoslavia as a subsidiary organ of the conference and was placed under the direction of the UNHCR. After the dissolution of the conference in January 1996 (and following the Dayton Agreement whose Annex 7 charged the UNHCR with elaborating a regional strategy aimed at the return to their homes of displaced persons following the break-up of Yugoslavia), it was simply attached to the Peace Implementation Council.

[17] See *Update on Durable Solutions for Refugees and Displaced Persons in the Context of the Dayton Agreement* (Working Group on Humanitarian Issues, document HIWG/99/5, 29 November 1999, p. 2, chart 1).

the Council of Europe, UNESCO, the Royaumont Process and also the Austrian, German, Bulgarian and Finnish Ministers of Education, its object was to co-ordinate co-operative efforts undertaken in the region in the medium and long term. Starting from the premise that education constitutes a privileged instrument for the promotion of tolerance and mutual understanding, the members of the Stability Pact considered that it was apt to use the structures of a 'Reinforced Graz Process' to encourage the peoples of the region, where the enemy is less a stranger than the close neighbour, to at last find a common language in particular through a revision of the teaching of history.[18]

As to the issue of interparliamentary co-operation it has been entrusted to the Process for Stability and Good Neighbourhood in South-Eastern Europe, also known as the Royaumont Process. Launched by France at Royaumont on 12 December 1995, this forum has developed into a laboratory for projects financed by the PHARE programme under the auspices of the European Union. Its role is to support the implementation of the civilian aspects of the Dayton Agreement by encouraging regional projects aimed at restoring confidence, good neighbourhood, cultural and scientific co-operation as well as freedom of movement and human contact between the civil societies of the countries of the region. The Stability Pact gave to the Royaumont Process the task of formulating a plan aimed at the development of an authentic parliamentarism in the countries of the region.[19]

Chaired by the Director-General of International Affairs of the Bank of Italy (Fabrizio Saccomanni) and co-chaired by the former Yugoslav Republic of Macedonia (FYROM) for the first six months of the year 2000, the Working Table on Reconstruction, Development and Economic Co-operation sat for the first time at Bari on 9 October 1999. It included in its programme of activities the following subjects: commercial questions, regional development, regional infrastructure, private sector development, co-operation with the private sector, elaboration of an investment Charter, navigation on the Danube and fight against corruption.[20] This list calls for three brief comments.

In the first place, the participants decided not to create *ad hoc* working structures, preferring to give direct responsibility to a number of international institutions already managing operational programmes in the region. Thus, the World Bank was tasked with establishing (in collaboration with the EIB) a global framework for regional development and investment projects, the EBRD with co-ordinating the demands submitted by the countries of the region in relation with the private sector, the EIB with assuring the co-ordination and evaluation of projects relating to regional infrastructure, and the SECI with setting up a regional 'Business Advisory Council' aimed at stimulating co-operation with the private

---

[18] The formulation 'Reinforced Graz Process' expresses the idea of a process implying an enlarged range of contributors and social partners – including the World Bank, the UN and the OCDE. The website of the Graz Process is: www.see-educoop.net
[19] The website of the Royaumont Process is: http://royaumont.lrf.gr
[20] Stability Pact *Official Texts*, op. cit., pp. 49–52.

sector.[21] Furthermore, the Danube Commission was mandated to study the problem (in fact more political than technical) of the re-establishment of shipping on the river. We can also note that the Table established a specific procedure for the consideration of projects relating to regional infrastructure and the private sector.

Secondly, the special interest in the economic dimension of the Stability Pact shown by Washington and London is noteworthy. The United States undertook to organise on their territory a high-level meeting tasked with proposing an Action Plan looking at the elimination of obstacles to intra-regional commercial exchange and also the accession to the WTO of the region's countries. As for the United Kingdom, it took on the task of elaborating (in co-operation with the relevant international organisations starting with the OCDE) a Charter on Investment including implementation and follow-up mechanisms.[22]

Thirdly, under American impulse, the fight against corruption has been included on the agenda. However, given that the general theme of good governance had to be considered by all three Working Tables, it was left to the Special Co-ordinator of the Stability Pact to take a decision on the relevant concrete measures to be undertaken on this matter.

Chaired by the Swedish State Secretary for Foreign Affairs (Jan Eliasson) and co-chaired by Bosnia and Herzegovina until 30 June 2000, the Working Table on Security Related Issues inaugurated its work at Oslo on 13 and 14 October 1999. Contrary to the two others, it decided to form two Sub-tables tackling respectively the external and domestic dimensions of security as follows:[23]

Questions concerning defence and security affairs	Questions concerning justice and home affairs
Arms control	Fight against corruption and organised crime
Confidence- and security-building measures (CSBMs): transparency of military budgets, development of military contacts, etc.	Police and judicial reform
Non-proliferation of arms (control of arms exports, including light weapons)	Migratory flows
De-mining	
Conflict prevention and crisis management	

---

[21] Created by the United States and the European Union at Geneva on 6 December 1996, and managed by the United Nations Economic Commission for Europe (ECE), the South-Eastern European co-operative Initiative (SECI) is a forum which aims to encourage economic co-operation between the countries of the region and to facilitate their integration into European structures. Its website is: www.unece.org/seci/

[22] On the basic elements of the Charter, see *Official Texts*, p. 41.

[23] See *Official Texts*, p. 53–58.

All the themes to be addressed by the defence and external security Sub-table come under OSCE competence, in particular (for the first four) the Forum for Security Co-operation – its specialised organ on politico-military aspects of security.[24] It is worth recalling that Annex 1-B of the Dayton Agreement on Regional Military Stabilisation, entrusted the OSCE with the task of elaborating and implementing three specific instruments: an agreement on CSBMs between the entities forming the Republic of Bosnia and Herzegovina (article II), an agreement on arms control concerning the Republic of Bosnia and Herzegovina, its two constitutive entities, Croatia and the FRY (article IV), and last but not least an arms control agreement concerning Yugoslavia and its neighbourhood ('*in and around Yugoslavia*', article V). The agreements relative to articles II and IV became operational in 1996,[25] whereas article V negotiations have only been under way since 1998. It is therefore clear that the activities of the Stability Pact relative to questions of external security will be conducted essentially through the OSCE. In the immediate future the organisation has been charged with setting up, under Austrian direction, an informal working group on the question of improving military contacts between the countries of the region, including through meetings at Ministers of Defence level.

One could judge that the inclusion of conflict prevention and crisis management on the agenda the defence and external security Sub-table is overly ambitious. In fact, the Sub-table's task here is just to consider the possibility of an enlargement of the composition of the peacekeeping force for South-Eastern Europe constituted in 1998 between Albania, Bulgaria, FYROM, Greece, Italy, Romania and Turkey.[26]

As to the agenda of the Sub-table on questions concerning justice and home affairs, its items (at least the first two) come under the recurrent theme of good governance. Their implementation requires joint action from a cluster of international institutions (OCDE, the UN, SECI, the Central European Initiative, the European Commission and so on) among which the OSCE and the Council of Europe because of their expertise will have to play a major role.[27]

The OSCE's Relation to the Stability Pact

Soon after the launching of the Stability Pact by the European Union, the OSCE demonstrated its willingness to make an outstanding contribution to the development and implementation of a process whose principles, norms and

---

[24] On the activities of the Forum, see our book: *L'OSCE dans l'Europe post-communiste, 1990–1996*, Brussels, Bruylant, 1996, pp. 148–221 and 559–604. See also OSCE document RC.GAL/175/99, 19 November 1999, pp. 57–69.
[25] On this point see *L'OSCE dans l'Europe post-communiste*, op. cit., pp. 568–572.
[26] For the text of the Agreement establishing the Force which was signed at Skopje on 26 September 1998 see, OSCE document SEC.DEL/232/98, 30 September 1998.
[27] The OSCE was especially charged with establishing a task force on the prevention of human trafficking.

objectives it fully shared. Hence decision 306 of its Permanent Council, adopted on 1 July 1999, placing the Stability Pact for South-Eastern Europe 'under the auspices of the OSCE'.[28]

Unilateral to all appearances, the decision could only have been made at the request of the European Union. Whatever the case, the precise practical meaning of the expression 'under the auspices of the OSCE' was not clearly specified. Considered in the light of the 1995 European Union's Stability Pact in Europe, which also has been placed under the auspices of the OSCE, it appeared somewhat ambiguous. Indeed, once that Pact was signed in Paris on 21 March 1995, the European Union gave up all responsibilities in regard to it by handing over all follow-up functions to the OSCE;[29] in other terms, the 1995 Stability Pact became part and parcel of OSCE activities.[30] In the case of the Stability Pact of 1999, the situation appears quite different. Although the Permanent Council's decision announced that the OSCE will 'work for compliance with the provisions of the Stability Pact by the Participating States, in accordance with its procedures and established principles' – meaning the integration of implementation activities within the OSCE – the Pact will nevertheless remain under the political direction of the European Union. It is logical to assume that the Stability Pact will be co-managed by both organisations under a certain division of labour. Thus, and as previously said, the Special Co-ordinator of the Stability Pact (whose appointment was made by the European Union after consultation with the OSCE Chairman-in-Office) has to provide 'periodic progress reports to the OSCE according to its procedures, on behalf of the South-Eastern Europe Regional Table'.[31]

Why did the European Union choose the OSCE and not another European institution (such as the Council of Europe) for the joint management of the Stability Pact process? The reasons are obvious. The OSCE is the only organisation whose mandate, based on comprehensive security, allows it to contribute to all three Working Tables of the Pact.[32] It is also the only security

---

[28] PC.DEC/306 of 1 July 1999.
[29] The OSCE accepted to assume that role through Decision 29 (23 March 1995) and Decision 63 (25 July 1995) of its Permanent Council.
[30] The 1999 Stability Pact has actually nothing to do with the 1995 Stability Pact. Despite a similar denomination, the two processes differ in their geographical scope, their objectives and their implementation mechanisms. Thus, the 1995 Pact concerned certain parts of Eastern and Central Europe as well as the Baltic region, whereas the 1999 Pact is applicable to South-Eastern Europe. Furthermore, while the 1995 Pact was conceived as a project of preventive diplomacy, the 1999 Pact has clearly post-conflict rehabilitation (or peace-building) objectives. The 1999 Pact, which includes elaborate structures, has also been conceived in a functional and operational perspective beyond any comparison with the 1995 Pact.
[31] PC.DEC/306 of 1 July 1999.
[32] The basic OSCE contribution concerns democratisation and human rights, and security-related issues. In the field of economic reconstruction, development and co-operation, the OSCE could only provide political support to efforts made by international economic and financial institutions.

organisation operationally active through field missions in four countries of the former Yugoslavia (Bosnia and Herzegovina, Croatia, the Former Yugoslav Republic of Macedonia and the Federal Republic of Yugoslavia/Kosovo) and Albania. Finally, and even more importantly, the 'owners' (or direct beneficiaries) of the Pact do not belong to the European Union while they do enjoy the status of full OSCE participating States: the OSCE offers the best place for monitoring the Pact's implementation and also the most suitable forum where a standing political pressure can be exerted upon the concerned countries for better compliance.[33] In any event, Decision 306 commits the OSCE to make use of its institutions and instruments and their expertise to contribute to the proceedings of the South-Eastern Regional Table and of the Working Tables, to host meetings of the Working Tables at the venue of its Permanent Council and to work in close co-operation with all interested international organisations and institutions to achieve the objectives set out in the Stability Pact.[34]

Through Decision 306, the OSCE also asked its Chairman-in-Office 'to promote further the development of the regional dimension of the OSCE's efforts in South-Eastern Europe through the use of the mechanisms of the Stability Pact'.[35] The Chairman-in-Office tasked the Head of the OSCE field mission in Bosnia and Herzegovina (United States Ambassador Robert Barry) for that purpose. The latter submitted an interim report (September 1999), followed by a final report which was handed over to the Istanbul Summit (November 1999).[36]

The Barry recommendations insisted on the crucial necessity of avoiding institutional duplication and overlap by means of an efficient OSCE–European Union division of labour, beginning with a close co-operation between the OSCE Chairman-in-Office and the Stability Pact Co-ordinator. Concerning the OSCE as such, they stressed that the challenge facing the latter was to make creative uses of existing channels of co-operation and communication among its missions as well as between individual missions and the OSCE's central institutions. The expansion of interface among the OSCE field missions in areas of common concern in order to avoid duplicative projects (citing as a relevant example the existing co-operation established between the OSCE field missions in Bosnia and Croatia to improve freedom of movement across borders and to organise elections) was accordingly recommended. But the improvement of 'lateral' communication and co-operation

---

[33] This is why Decision 306 states that the OSCE will 'work for compliance' with the provisions of the Stability Pact by its participating States.
[34] PC.DEC/306 of 1 July 1999.
[35] PC.DEC/306 of 1 July 1999.
[36] See 'The Development of an OSCE Regional Approach for Southeastern Europe' (CIO.GAL/66/99 of 3 September 1999) and 'The Development of the Southeastern Europe Regional Dimension of the OSCE' (CIO.GAL/83/99 0f 10 November 1999). The idea of an OSCE regional dimension was stimulated but not directly inspired by the launching of the Stability Pact. Indeed, it was already concretely discussed in a routine annual co-ordinating meeting of OSCE Heads of field missions held in Oslo at the beginning of 1999.

among the field missions was to be considered as only one side of the coin – the other side being measures aiming at a more closer integration of the efforts of those field missions and of the OSCE central institutions. In his final report, Ambassador Barry also recommended that the Chairman-in-Office should appoint a personal representative for regional issues counting on the services of a small support group to be established in the Vienna Secretariat with earmarked financial resources.

The Istanbul Summit Declaration recognised the 'leading role' of the European Union within the Stability Pact process, confirmed the willingness of the OSCE to play a 'key role' in that process and tasked the Permanent Council to develop a 'regional strategy' to support its aims.[37] Subsequently, in March 2000, the OSCE Permanent Council adopted a Regional Strategy for South-Eastern Europe whose main elements included: increased co-operation and co-ordination between OSCE field Missions in the area, increased co-operation with other interested international organisations on the basis of the Istanbul 'Platform for Co-operative Security', assistance to the Stability Pact 'owners' in implementing OSCE commitments and obligations, development of OSCE regional projects and execution of projects requested by the Stability Pact.[38] In sum, as Ambassador Barry put it in his final report, the expansion of the OSCE regional dimension in South-Eastern Europe is becoming an organisational priority for 2000, both on its own merits and because it will contribute to the Stability Pact's success.

Conclusion

Contrary to some press reports, the Stability Pact is not supposed to be a 'Marshall Plan for the Balkans'. In contrast to the Marshall Plan, it appears as a project basically conceived and financed by the Europeans. Moreover, it is targeted at a politically heterogeneous and divided region whose endogenous actors have neither the will nor the capacity to create on their own a collective political dynamic. Nevertheless, by its goals as well as by its approach, the Pact appears as an original and welcome enterprise. Founded on the gamble of 'de-Balkanising' (that is to say 'Europeanising') the Balkans, this enterprise proposes an integrated and co-ordinated operational response to the overall problems of a structurally unstable region. More precisely, the Pact aims at bringing a durable solution to the endemic political conflicts of South-Eastern Europe by addressing not only their symptoms but also the deep underlying economic, social and human root-causes. Its approach moreover illustrates the new partner relationships that have developed

---

[37] Paragraph 11 of the Istanbul Summit Declaration.
[38] PC.DEC/344 of 16 March 2000. Decision 344 was drafted on the basis of a 'Work Plan for the OSCE Regional Strategy for Southeastern Europe' initially submitted by the Norwegian Chairman-in-Office before the Istanbul Summit (CIO.GAL/73/99 of 13 October 1999).

between the international organisations in Europe since the Dayton Agreement. The Stability Pact process operates both as a main co-ordinating organ and a laboratory for new ideas: its concern is as much to increase the efficiency of existing programs in other multilateral settings as to favour the adoption of new projects. Pushing the multilateral co-operation structures operationally active in the region to work in union on the basis of their respective 'comparative advantages', it constitutes a significant application of the Platform for Co-operative Security which forms an integral part of the European Security Charter adopted by the OSCE at Istanbul on 19 November 1999.[39]

---

[39] For an analysis of the Platform see our contribution on the Istanbul Charter in this volume.

Chapter 10

The Co-operation between International Organisations in the Management of the Third Yugoslav War

Eric Remacle

Rather than the perilous exercise of drawing up an exhaustive list of the eight and a half years of war in the Balkans, this contribution will be more modest, presenting ten propositions on the lessons of the involvement of international organisations in what can be called 'the third Balkan war'.

I

It seems necessary to resituate the conflicts which have bloodied the territory of former Yugoslavia since 1991 in a longer context, as proposed by the method of the historian Fernand Braudel. We can consider the recent conflict as the extension of the two previous Balkan wars of this century: that of the 1940s and that of the 1910s, or even from as far back as the birth of the Balkan Nation States after the carving up of the Ottoman Empire in the nineteenth century. In the same vein as Eric Hobsbawm, who in his work *The Age of Extremes. The Short Twentieth Century* invites us to understand the period 1914–45 as a single world war interrupted by a twenty-year truce, one can indeed, with the passage of time, remark that the wars of South-Eastern Europe constitute a long conflict of nearly a century interrupted by a few periods of peace. The similarities are indeed striking. The same projection of identity into the territories, the same confrontation between competing nationalist tendencies, the same ferocity of combat, the same alliances between belligerents and Great Powers, the same sort of external intervention, the same mobilisation of multiple forms of propaganda by the two camps, the same type of international settlement involving types of protectorates. To remark this is not to attempt to condemn the region and its people to a sort of war fatalism, as certain paternalist commentators have tried to do in Western Europe these last eight years. It is more a question of identifying the deeply rooted double-sided nature of this conflict. On one hand at a local level the struggle for the creation of mono-ethnic Nation States; on the other the geopolitical reorganisation of the European order by Cold War's victorious powers.

II

But a long-term interpretation of history need not lead one to believe in determinism or in the unchanging character of history. On the contrary, the framework in which the war of the 1990s has unfolded appears wholly unique and specific, particularly due to the end of the Cold War and the subsequent geopolitical readjustment leading to the reinforcement of the American superpower, a considerably weakened Russia, the tentative emergence of Europe, and an increased weight for the Muslim world on the international scene. In comparison with the nineteenth century or the first half of the twentieth century the observer is struck by the existence henceforth of a multilateralism at the same time both extremely elaborate and riddled with contradictions. The *Sainte Alliance* and European Concert of the nineteenth century gave way to the United Nations, nonetheless it was a Contact Group, which Metternich himself would have been proud of, who finally played the major diplomatic role. The competing military alliances such as the Triple Entente, the Triple alliance or the 'Petite Entente' or even more recently the Warsaw Pact and NATO have passed into the recesses of history. However, today it is the last of these alliances, a deeply transformed and reworked global actor, which brings iron and fire to Balkan sores to impose *Pax Americana*. The end of the twentieth century wavers between a new multilateralism and the renaissance of the Concert of Powers.

III

Thus a theoretical approach which divides the actors into local belligerents behaving with an irrational ethnic-tribal mentality, and the wise international community neutral and bringer of peace, is unsatisfactory. In fact an empirical analysis of the different stages of the conflict highlights a dynamic of local, regional and world dimensions creating a system of complex interactions between the parties to the conflict, the Great Powers and international organisations. An examination of three examples should be convincing.

The first is that of the strange dialectic between the fighting on the ground for the conquest of territory and the maps of the many peace plans discussed at the tables of diplomatic negotiations. How many times did the belligerents try to conquer a certain territory to be better placed in the negotiations, or did the international negotiators propose new maps adapted to the territorial gains of one party or another?

The second example concerns the arming and disarming of the parties, perceived by the Great Powers and the international organisations as an issue even more than the resolution of the conflict. How else to explain the multitude of violations and bypasses of the weapons embargoes by countries which themselves had announced these embargoes at the UN, the OSCE or the EU? The tip of this iceberg was without doubt the unilateral US decision to cease participation in the monitoring of the Adriatic Sea embargo in November 1994, leading to an historically unique communiqué of protestation from the WEU. It must be stated that throughout the conflict, up to and including the recent Kosovo phase, Americans, Europeans, Russians and Muslim countries have shamelessly stocked the arsenals of the belligerents that they respectively supported. A strange international community indeed which turns out to be both referee and player in so-called 'crisis management'.

Finally, the third example is about a war of labels, data and pictures. An extraordinary diplomatic and media mobilisation surrounded the labelling of a particular stage of the conflict as an 'aggression', 'genocide' or 'human catastrophe', or around the calculation of the number of victims and their presumed nationality. It is perhaps above all at this level, involving prodigious propaganda efforts on all sides to conquer public opinions, that wars are won and lost. Here also a long historic perspective shows that such is the way with all wars.

IV

Let us now dissect the conflict of these last few years as a function of the action of international organisations. Without entering into the details this can be analysed *grosso modo* in five phases, each representing not only a chronological stage but also an international intervention model, having a different internal logic and a different relative weighting of local or international actors resulting in different outcomes.

The first model corresponds to the period between June and October 1991, when the European Union tried to monopolise the international action with the support of the CSCE. The Community succeeded in gaining the role of peacemaker but failed to agree on the deployment of a WEU peacekeeping force.

The second model corresponds more or less to the period from October 1991 to December 1993 and is characterised by the tandem between the European Community and the United Nations. This model subdivides into two variants.

- Variant A: the United Nations handles the military aspects, that is ceasefire negotiations and the deployment of UNPROFOR, while the Europeans lead the diplomatic process and take different measures towards different Yugoslav republics using both sanctions and recognition of independence. This variant characterises the end of the Croatian war between October 1991 and February 1992.
- Variant B: the United Nations, no longer restricting its action to peacekeeping, shares with the Community the diplomatic role of co-president of the peace conference and also takes steps in favour of certain belligerents and against others. The other international organisations CSCE, NATO and the WEU rally to the cause, above all for the application and monitoring of sanctions. This

model held true above all from the London Conference of August 1992 until the end of 1993 and applied to the management of the Bosnian conflict.

The third model is that of the Contact Group and NATO, supported by the Security Council, controlling operations. The Contact Group led the diplomatic dance and came up with a policy of 'carrot and stick' towards the conflicting parties. NATO was charged with peace-enforcement through such concepts as the 'no-fly zone', 'safe areas' and 'close air support', whereas the UN remained on the ground theoretically neutral and submitted to the hazards of a complex chain of command and of a NATO–UN 'dual key' revealing tensions between the Great Powers. The CSCE and the European Union were relegated to a secondary role focusing on sanctions and humanitarian aid. This was the dominant model from the beginning of 1994 until the Dayton Agreement.

The fourth model is one of international administrations or protectorates resulting from co-operation between interlocking institutions. The peacekeeping is assured by NATO, the administrative tasks, reconstruction and civil police are assured by a civilian High Representative, chosen *de facto* within the European Union which gives financial aid. The OSCE sees its role reinforced concerning election matters, military stabilisation, human rights and democratisation. This is the model applied for the administration of Bosnia and Herzegovina and Kosovo. It is strangely reminiscent of the protectorate project in Macedonia at the beginning of the century, never realised by the Great Powers. It is nevertheless possible that it will be transposed onto Montenegro and Macedonia if they happen to be also dragged into the war.

Finally the fifth model is that of coercive action led by NATO alone against one of the belligerents without a Security Council mandate, as we have recently seen.

The choice of one or other of these models will never be neutral, or inspired simply by the quest for efficiency, but is more the result of external actors' agendas, inspired either by a fear of the extension of the conflict, or by post-Cold War power struggles. It would be interesting to explore in detail each of these models, but that cannot be done here, since it would constitute a research programme, lasting many years, for all our institutes united. Put bluntly, according to the choice of a particular type of international action, the vanquers and the vanquished are not the same. Different power relationships would have led to a different chronological evolution and ultimately to a different outcome. Imagine for example that the 1993 Owen–Stoltenberg plan had been accepted by the Sarajevo Parliament and supported by the United States: then the UN–European Union duo would have been considered the most suitable to resolve regional conflicts, and not the Contact Group and NATO. Europe today would certainly not be as it is.

V

Behind the apparent confusion over the relations between the international organisations lies a power struggle between the actors around three key questions. Who has the legitimacy? What is law? Who has the force? These three questions nestle behind each apparently confused situation, behind each apparent lack of rationality in the roles of the organisations. Why the confusion of roles between civil and military organisations? Why the fog surrounding the definition of the mandating and mandated organisations? Why does NATO play a humanitarian role and why does the Council of Europe play one of soft security? Why suddenly create the Contact Group in 1994? Why did the US who at the beginning of the 1990s limited the OSCE's role, give it a new impetus with the Dayton Agreement? Why such a plethora of international mediators in the Former Yugoslavia Republic of Macedonia? Why in the same texts do we find references to Yugoslavia territorial integrity and a different treatment of Montenegro or Kosovo? Why place the Stability Pact, an EU initiative, under the auspices of the OSCE? Why did China vote against the maintenance of the UN Blue Helmets in Macedonia at the beginning of 1999, opening the way for the stationing of only NATO troops in this country? Such questions find a response only if we examine the issues of legitimacy, of law and of force and their effect on the behaviour of local and international actors. They will not be examined here. Let us be content to continue our proposition: the action of international organisations can only be interpreted if we take into account the will of their own member States to instrumentalise them. Realism is definitely not dead in international relations and Morgenthau's 'International politics, like all politics, is a struggle for power' is as relevant as always.

VI

However, a reading of the international action in the crisis can not be undertaken exclusively through a realist interpretation. As brilliantly summed up by the contemporary theoricien of international relations Ken Booth, Morgenthau's phrase should be examined the other way round to give a more complete understanding of the world. Thus today more apt is 'The struggle for power, like all politics, is world politics'. In other words a realist interpretation is part of a larger theoretical approach which sees world politics as a whole, integrating State and non-State actors, social classes and economic forces, regional and international organisations. In this context the nature of multilateralism seems to always produce more principles, norms, procedures, regimes and institutions, as if world politics followed the laws of thermodynamics and tried to counterbalance the entropic force of chaos by a negentropism of order and organisations. As stated by our colleague from University College, London, Jean Barréa, each crisis generates a surplus of crisis utopism, utopic attempts to construct new organisations which it is hoped will prevent subsequent crises. The Yugoslav crisis was no exception to this trend. It illustrated extraordinary human inventiveness in the creation of institutions and new concepts. It was during and in reaction to this crisis that we got the Badinter Commission, the EC Monitoring Mission, the SAMCOMM, the new OSCE instruments such as the High Commissioner for National Minorities, the field Missions, and the Court for Conciliation and Arbitration, the Blue Helmets, both humanitarian and preventive, the two Stability Pacts for Central Europe and South-Eastern Europe, the concepts of preventive diplomacy, of co-operative security, of peace-building, not to mention the traditional peace conferences. In short the Yugoslav crisis confirmed the massive investment of States and non-State actors in the constitution of a galaxy of institutions which substituted for the traditional power constellation. In the same vein, the centre of gravity of the world politics is continually moving towards the international organisations, the control of which becomes the crucial issue. Thus a 'new' non-hierarchic multilateralism emerges, structured in the form of a network. The study of networks in organisational sociology teaches us that they do not connect any more through hierarchical power, but depend on a capacity for influence, through relationship strategies between the actors. In other words, networks are in essence no more democratic than hierarchies, they are just differently organised and the power is distributed by different sets of rules. The same is true for interlocking institutional networks: some are more influential than others, in this case it is the Great Western Powers around which are organised a series of concentric circles: Contact Group, Permanent Security Council Members, G-8, NATO, European Union, Euro-Atlantic Partnership Council, OSCE and so on. The issue then becomes to know who sits at the centre of the web. From this point of view the hypothesis 'EU first' met with hardly any success in 1991, the scenario 'OSCE first' once evoked never represented a consensus within the OSCE itself, the approach 'UN first' has been thrown into question by powerful regional organisation. The only remaining option is thus 'NATO first', made possible by three steps taken by the Americans which materialised in 1999. These were the bypassing of the UN Security Council, the proposition of a 'subsidiarity' between NATO and the OSCE to the benefit of the former and the expectancy of a right of Atlantic 'first refusal' in the case of purely European action in crisis management.

VII

In these networks of the new multilateralism, a novel actor tried to assert itself: the European Union. From this point of view the EU not only influenced the unfolding of the Yugoslav crises, but was itself changed by the crisis. There are many manifestations of this interdependence between 1991 and 1999. The Franco-German proposition of an intervention force between Serbs and Croats in Croatia is better understood by the parallel negotiations of the Maastricht Treaty and its chapter on the CFSP than by a real willingness from Bonn or Paris to intervene on the ground. The same applies to the first stretching of the EU wings regarding the embryonic CFSP in this war, for example when introducing the employment of special envoys and testing a closer relationship with the WEU. Or the two examples where the Yugoslav crisis in 1993 and 1999 led the Union to propose the signature of regional Stability Pacts for Central and South-Eastern Europe. Or in spring 1995 when the French President proposed the idea of a European Rapid Reaction Force destined to protect the Blue Helmets and to open up the Sarajevo enclave, in order that Europe might at least prove its existence on the military level beside the US and NATO during the last weeks of the Bosnian war. Lastly, when the Kosovo crisis provoked an acceleration of the debate on European defence and increased pressure for EU enlargement not only for the CEECs and Cyprus but also for Turkey and the Balkan countries.

VIII

The fact remains that the European Union is a contradictory actor because it is composed of multiple actors and institutions at various different levels. These contradictions are manifestly evident in such circumstances. How indeed could the Community, after the Brioni Accords of 1991 and all through the conflict, try to contain the conflict while fuelling it by legitimising the intention of certain republics to become independent? How could it generate the essential diplomatic solutions contained in the peace plans, while allowing itself to be deposed *in fine* by the United States? How could it at the same time criticise the American concept of rogue States when applied to Cuba, Iran and Libya, and approve it when applied to Serbia? How could it refer to the principles of the Rule of Law and the role of the United Nations in its own founding treaty and at the same time support an illegal NATO military action not covered by the UN? Why did it abandon midway the inter-institutional co-operation model which had given it its most significant role, its tandem with the UN in 1992 and 1993? And why in the six years since the CFSP has existed has there never been a single common position relative to the EU's UN policy?

IX

It is true that these contradictions were not only true for the European Union. They also apply to the failures and incoherence of NATO during 1994, or the amazing absence of United States participation in UNPROFOR between 1992 and 1995, today consigned to forgotten history because NATO and the United States won the war. These are none the less crucial elements in the history of the conflict. We are far from having looked at all these multiple contradictions. Such as the decision to rapidly call elections in Bosnia which resulted in a legitimisation of the most nationalist leaders, some of whom were subsequently relieved of their responsibilities by the High Representative because of their nationalist policies. Or such as calls for sub-regional integration, of which the first manifestation was not the signature of multilateral accords, but bilateral ones between the European Union and each State in the region. The objective of stability was ambiguous from the outset if we consider the list of manifest contributions to the destabilisation of the region by external actors.

X

Then, we have to wonder about the causes of these contradictions. In attributing them to the power struggles between the actors, and to the new centre of gravity which is constituted by the international organisations in world politics, we have identified what are very probably some important sources. But the world can not be seen only through a positivist vision attached uniquely to the interests of disembodied rational actors. Politics is first of all led by human beings with values and preconceptions, thus obliging us to adopt a cognitive approach. Why indeed have we seen these last years in Western cultures a strong re-legitimisation of the use of force as a solution to the world's problems? Why has a sort of implicit right to secession resulted in a proliferation of States – as it happens, weak States surrounded by regional and world powers? Why lastly has the recourse to protectorates been largely accepted by public opinion, which not long ago was averse to anything which smacked of colonialism? To investigate this deep ideological change in our own societies is without doubt another task for today's academics. And so perhaps the main lesson of the War in Yugoslavia is that we are obliged firstly and foremost to reflect on ourselves.

Chapter 11

The 1999 Istanbul Charter for European Security: A Critical Assessment

Victor-Yves Ghebali

Bringing to an end the work started in March 1995 for the purpose of a Common and Comprehensive Security Model for Europe for the Twenty-First Century, the OSCE adopted at its fourth post-Cold War Summit (Istanbul 18–19 November 1999) a Charter for European Security. Starting from an analysis of the risks and challenges to the security of post-Communist Europe ('Our Common Challenges', paragraphs 2–6) and a reaffirmation of pan-European principles ('Our Common Foundations', paragraphs 7–11), that instrument provides for the strengthening of the structures of the OSCE ('Our Common Response', paragraphs 12–33) and, more particularly, of its operational capacities ('Our Common Instruments', paragraphs 34–47) before finally offering, in an appended 'Platform for Co-operative Security', guidelines for a new partnership co-operation with other security organisations.

The Charter is certainly not an empty shell. As predicted by the European Union's countries, its does have a substantial 'added value'. Furthermore, its wording avoids esoteric jargon.[1] However, due to numerous political differences between Russia (supported only by Belarus) and the other countries of the OSCE, the elaboration of the Charter was not an easy task. The final product cannot be appreciated without due reference to the Russian positions and proposals.

This chapter offers an analysis of the Charter from four perspectives: politico-military issues, institutional issues, operational capacities for conflict prevention and crisis management and, lastly, interface with other international security organisations.

Politico-Military Issues

From the start of the Security Model exercise which preceded the drafting of the Charter, the participating States realised that they could not agree on the modalities of an appropriate strengthening of the operational capacities of the OSCE without

---

[1] During a meeting of the Security Model Committee the United States expressed clearly their firm opposition to any text 'which would require a Ph.D. in Political Science to understand' (PC.SMC/150/99 of 27 September 1999).

identifying beforehand the risks and challenges prevailing in the OSCE area. On the basis of the views expressed by the Governments in 1995, the Hungarian Presidency established an initial list corresponding to each of the OSCE's three sectors of activities: the politico-military dimension, the economic and environmental dimension, and the human dimension. The elaboration of that list showed that the perception of Russia (focused on NATO enlargement) and that of a number of other Governments (pointing to the stationing of foreign military forces without specific consent of the host nation, or the use of the control of energy as means of political pressure by certain States) were far from being convergent. In the course of the updating efforts undertaken under the leadership of successive Presidencies of the OSCE from 1996 onwards, the participating States arrived at the conclusion that the transnational, mixed character (both internal and external) and evolving nature of these risks and challenges made an exhaustive list impossible.

For that reason, the Istanbul Charter does not contain any systematic listing. It only mentions international terrorism, violent extremism, organised crime and drug trafficking as 'growing challenges to security', and the uncontrolled spread of small arms and light weapons as 'a threat to peace and security' (paragraph 4). Besides, it acknowledges that 'acute economic problems and environmental degradation' may have serious implications for the security in the OSCE area (paragraph 5). Finally, it recognises that instability in the neighbouring area of the Mediterranean and in areas in direct proximity to participating States such as Central Asia 'creates challenges that directly affect the security and prosperity of OSCE states' (paragraph 5).

Due to Moscow's opposition, no express references to the stationing of foreign troops without the consent of the host State were included.[2] This 'negative' Russian victory does not compensate for the fact the Charter contains no provisions concerning the security interests of States not belonging to a military alliance or the non-deployment of nuclear weapons on territories where there are presently none – all the more that it clearly reaffirms 'the inherent right of each and every participating State to be free to choose or change its security arrangements, including treaties of alliance, as they evolve' (paragraph 8). The Charter does recognise that 'each participating State has an equal right to security', that participating States 'will not strengthen their security at the expense of the security of other States' and that 'no State, group of States or organisation can have any pre-eminent responsibility for maintaining peace and stability in the OSCE area or can consider any part of the OSCE area as its sphere of influence'

---

[2] However, paragraph 19 of the Istanbul Summit Declaration commits Russia to a 'complete withdrawal of the Russian forces from the territory of Moldova by the end of 2002'.

(paragraph 8). This terminology is, however, double-edged: if it allows Russia an anti-NATO reading, it purports at the same time to have an implied condemnation of the Russian concept of 'near abroad'.

It is also worthwhile mentioning that, in response to the concern of small countries (such as Malta), the Istanbul Charter embodies an emerging mild security guarantee. Developing an idea vaguely formulated in the 1994 Code of Conduct on Politico-Military Aspects of Security, paragraph 16 of the Charter commits OSCE governments 'to consult promptly ... with a participating State seeking assistance in realising its right to individual or collective self-defence in the event that its sovereignty, territorial integrity and political independence are threatened', in order to 'consider jointly the nature of the threat and actions that may be required' in defence of the OSCE's common values.

Although human dimension questions fall outside the scope of politico-military issues, mention should be made of a provision of the Charter which specifically deals with national minorities. Paragraph 19 is indeed noteworthy since it states that the full respect for the rights of persons belonging to national minorities 'besides being an end in itself, may not undermine, but strengthen territorial integrity and sovereignty'; it has also the merit of recalling that 'various concepts of autonomy' together with other positive approaches enumerated in the OSCE's 1992 Geneva Expert Meeting Report remain relevant. Paragraph 19 reflects some unusual degree of consensus on a matter which is normally divisive among the participating States.

Institutional Issues

In this particular area, the Istanbul Charter hardly responds to Moscow's expectations. Throughout the debates concerning the Security Model and later on in the debates on the Charter itself, Russia raised three major demands. First, it pleaded for a full-fledged rationalisation of OSCE structures based on a formal distinction between 'Principal Organs' and 'Special Institutions'. Such a rationalisation implied not only the reinforcement of already existing bodies (the Secretariat or the Forum for Security Co-operation), but also the creation of new organs: a Council of Heads of State or Government combining the present functions of OSCE Summits and Review Meetings as well as a Committee on Political Security attached to the current Permanent Council. Second, Russia argued that the OSCE's decisions ought to become binding (as a first step towards the attribution of legal foundations to the OSCE) and, at the same time, excluding the 'consensus minus one' rule under which Yugoslavia was suspended in 1992. Third, Russia requested the institutionalisation of the Security Model Committee, the negotiating body of the Charter, on the ground that the latter needed ongoing revision to adapt to changing political realities in Europe.

Motivated by a real concern for not jeopardising the OSCE's outstanding flexibility, all the other States except Belarus refused to follow Moscow on the first point. The Charter therefore does not prescribe an institutional overhaul. To the contrary, it confirms the dichotomy – considered unhappy by some delegations – between the general political functions of the Permanent Council and the exclusively politico-military competencies of the Forum for Security Co-operation (paragraph 34). However, it establishes a new informal open-ended body (the Preparatory Committee) whose task is to assist the OSCE's Permanent Council to adopt decisions with more transparency and through a wider political consultation process (paragraph 35). For reasons of urgency or of political opportunism, the practice of consultation used in the Permanent Council does not normally involve the small delegations until the last stage: the establishment of a Preparatory Committee is thus supposed to remedy a notoriously unsatisfactory situation.

Moscow's second demand has not been totally ignored: paragraph 10 of the Charter confirms the continuation of consensus 'as the basis for OSCE decision-making' but without specifically excluding the use of the 'consensus minus one' procedure.

As to the third Russian demand, it was put aside by means of a provision taking stock of 'the completion of the work of the Security Model Committee' (paragraph 51).

Two brief remarks remain to be made in connection with institutional issues. First, paragraph 17 of the Charter recognises that the Parliamentary Assembly (which is not a statutory organ of the OSCE, but a forum composed of parliamentarians from OSCE countries) 'has developed into one of the most important OSCE institutions ..., particularly in the field of democratic development and election monitoring': beyond its face value, this tribute – most unusual from an intergovernmental body towards an inter-parliamentary organ – suggests that competition between the Warsaw Office and the Parliamentary Assembly in the field of election monitoring is no longer a problem. Second, in paragraph 18, the Charter recognises that 'difficulties can arise from the absence of a legal capacity of the Organisation' and, therefore, announces that the participating States 'will seek to improve the situation' in this regard. Included at the insistence of France this provision signals that the debate over the granting of a legal capacity to the OSCE has been formally reopened.

Operational Capacities for Conflict Prevention and Crisis Management

The provisions related to the strengthening of the OSCE's operational capacities represent the real 'added value' of the Istanbul Charter. They concern three specific points: Peacekeeping Operations, Long-Term Missions and 'Joint Co-operative Actions'.

Peacekeeping Operations (PKOs)

Although a large set of specific provisions on peacekeeping was included in Chapter III of the Helsinki Document 1992, the issue of PKOs remained a sensible issue within the OSCE. During the elaboration of the Istanbul Charter, three competing approaches were presented. The first, defended by the United States, argued that the OSCE had neither the expertise nor the practical capacity necessary to mount its own PKOs: as a consequence, the OSCE should limit itself to provide an exclusively non-military contribution to PKOs deployed under the aegis of other international organisations. Russia rejected this concept as leaving a *de facto* politico-military monopoly to NATO in Europe and recalled that the Helsinki Document 1992 authorised the OSCE to undertake its own PKOs; however, it maintained (with no legal firm ground) that the latter could only be deployed on the basis of a UN Security Council resolution in order to avoid the perception that such an operation be of a coercive type or serve the interests of a 'limited group of States'. Between these two extremes positions, the European Union countries took the middle ground affirming that it was judicious to leave all options open, that is, not to exclude a priori the case where the OSCE could be the most appropriate institution to set up a PKO.

At an initial glance the EU seems to have won the day since paragraph 46 of the Istanbul Charter acknowledges that the OSCE could not only play a direct 'leading role' in peacekeeping, but also 'provide the mandate covering peacekeeping by others and seek the support of participating States as well as other organisations to provide resources and expertise'. Actually, paragraph 46 has been drafted in particularly restrictive terms. Thus, it only announces the decision of the participating States 'to *explore* options for a *potentially* greater and wider role for the OSCE in peacekeeping'. After reaffirming (as requested by Russia) the rights and obligations of the participating States under the UN Charter, the same provision does not go beyond confirming that 'the OSCE can, on a *case-by-case basis* and by consensus, decide to play *a role* in peacekeeping, including a leading role *when participating States judge it* to be the most effective and appropriate organisation'. Moreover, an analysis of other provisions of the Istanbul Charter (those relative to police activities and to the REACT concept) shows that the American approach aimed at limiting the OSCE to purely civil tasks has prevailed.

Paragraph 44 of the Charter commits the participating States to reinforce the role of the OSCE in civilian police-related activities aimed at conflict prevention, crisis management and post-conflict rehabilitation. According to the Charter, activities of this type – already undertaken in Croatia by the OSCE – could imply police monitoring (for example in view of preventing police from carrying out possible discriminatory activities based on religious and ethnic identity) and police training aimed at improving the tactical and operational capacities of local police services, reforming paramilitary forces, providing policing skills to fight organised crime (anti-drug, anti-corruption, anti-terrorist), creating multi-ethnic police services and so on.

Paragraph 42 of the Charter, which endorses the American-proposed concept of Rapid Expert Assistance and Co-operation Teams (REACT), goes in the same direction. Those teams will be composed of civil personnel and of police specialists, and will be called upon to intervene before certain problems degenerate into crises and to manage a crisis or to contribute to the rightful implementation of a recently-signed peace accord. Such teams would allow the rapid deployment of the civil component of a PKO (launched in all probability by other organisations considering paragraph 46 as examined above) or could serve as 'surge capacity to assist the OSCE with the rapid deployment of large-scale or specialised operations'. The availability at a national level of mobilisable REACT experts on demand is not just a formal promise: paragraph 35 of the Istanbul Summit Declaration engages the participating States 'to make this concept fully operational at the shortest possible time' and to implement it 'as a matter of priority'. Furthermore, the Charter provides for a special Operation Centre to be established within the Conflict Prevention Centre; served by a core of staff competent in all the domains of OSCE activity; the function of this centre will be to plan and deploy operations on the ground, notably those calling upon REACT experts.

Long-Term Missions (LTMs)

The Istanbul Charter has not introduced outstanding new elements concerning the field Missions which have been established on a case-by-case basis by the OSCE since 1992 in the Balkans, the Caucasus, Central Asia and the Baltic area as well as Central and Eastern Europe. However, in its paragraph 38 and on the basis of the experience gained so far, it offers a non-exhaustive list (the first of its kind) of the functions which the LTMs are expected to fulfil on the ground. Depending on the circumstances, an LTM (acting alone or in co-ordination with other international organisations) may be called upon to provide expert assistance and advice (professional training, election monitoring, implementation of practical projects and so on), especially for the consolidation of democratic institutions. It may also assume a 'good offices' or mediation role by facilitating the peaceful settlement of conflicts and verifying and/or assisting the fulfilment of agreements related thereto. It may equally provide support for post-conflict rehabilitation purposes. In any case, the LTMs are called upon to reinforce, when appropriate, the specific capacities and expertise of host countries in order to facilitate 'an efficient transfer of the tasks of the operation, and consequently the closure of the field operation' (paragraph 41).

Joint Co-operative Actions

As to the Polish concept of joint co-operative actions to be taken in response to situations of major violation of OSCE commitments or of a collapse of public order (as witnessed in Albania), the Charter does not go as far as envisaged by its proponents. The idea of assistance provided upon request to States experiencing structural difficulties in applying their undertakings posed no problem. Difficulties did arise with the suggestion that sanctions could be applied in the case of a refusal of such aid and, also, that the OSCE could intervene in a situation of public order collapse in the absence of a legitimate State authority. Concerned by NATO's unilateral military intervention in Kosovo and determined to avoid any possibility of the OSCE meddling in the handling of its Chechnya policy, Russia opposed any innovating provision increasing the authority of the OSCE in the internal affairs of its participating States: hence, the emphasis of the Istanbul Charter on the specific consent of the host State. Thus, paragraph 14 allows OSCE governments to take 'joint measures based on co-operation' in order to offer, when needed, 'assistance to participating States to enhance their compliance with OSCE principles and commitments'. In even more timid terms, paragraph 15 expresses the intention of governments only to 'consider ways of helping participating States requesting assistance in cases of internal breakdown of law and order' within the framework of a joint examination of 'the nature of the situation and possible ways and means of providing support to the State in question'.

Interface with Other Security Organisations

The Istanbul Charter includes, as an integral part, an annex entitled 'Operational Document – the Platform for Co-operative Security'. Initially proposed by the European Union, this text proceeds from the premise that the risks and challenges of post-Communist Europe cannot be met by a single State or organisation. Consequently, the Platform's rationale is the strengthening and development of closer co-operation with the organisations contributing to the various dimensions of comprehensive security in the OSCE area (European organisations, European sub-regional groupings and the United Nations bodies and Agencies) in order to avoid duplication and ensure efficient use of available international resources. Aiming at developing institutional co-operation on the basis of full equality and shared values, it clearly rules out the establishment of any kind of hierarchy or a permanent division of labour.

The Platform consists of a number of general 'principles and commitments' offered to those international organisations which evolve in political 'transparency' and whose membership is based on 'openness and free will' – and also whose member States, collectively or individually, adhere to the undertakings of the United Nations Charter and the fundamental OSCE instruments, fulfil their arms control/disarmament/CSBMs obligations and are prepared to deploy institutional resources in support of the OSCE's work in general, and more particularly in the fields of conflict prevention and management. In view of increasing inter-institutional understanding of existing conflict prevention tools, the OSCE proposes to organisations accepting the Platform regular contacts and meetings, the designation of liaison officers, the establishment of points of contact and cross-representation at appropriate meetings. Special meetings at political, executive and/or working level are also suggested to co-ordinate policies, determine areas of co-operation and address the modalities of such co-operation. Concerning field operations, the Platform calls for regular information exchanges and meetings, joint needs assessment missions, secondment of experts, appointment of liaison officers, development of common projects and operations, and joint training efforts. In regard to possible co-operative responses to specific crises, the OSCE offers to serve as 'a flexible framework for co-operation of the various mutually reinforcing efforts'. Lastly, the Platform charges the Secretary-General to prepare an annual report on 'interaction between organisations and institutions in the OSCE area'.

The ultimate *raison d'être* of the Platform is the development in the OSCE area of a 'culture' of co-operation between international organisations pursuing analogous or complementary goals. In itself the objective can hardly be said to be a revolutionary one. However, considered in the light of the institutional competition which has characterised the first post-Cold War years, it is timely and relevant. In the greater Europe, where several security institutions exist and are often requested to react simultaneously, the mutual acceptance of a minimum of formal common rules is certainly a positive event. Actually, and as demonstrated by the joint implementation of the Dayton Agreement by a range of international organisations on the basis of comparative advantage, synergetic co-operation has become, since 1996, a regular trend in the OSCE area. From this perspective, the Istanbul Platform presents a real merit: it codifies the basic rules of what may be called an 'institutional armistice'.

Conclusion

Evidently, the substance of the Istanbul Charter on European Security is much less far-reaching than one could reasonably have expected given the number of innovative proposals tabled during the drafting process. Yet, the Charter represents one of the major texts of the post-Cold War OSCE. Its main merit has to do with the fact that its substantial core is more operational than normative; it bears witness to the growing political relevance in Europe of an otherwise low-profile organisation which in, the same year, has also updated its CSBMs regime (Vienna Document 1999), established in Kosovo a field Mission totalling several thousand people and accepted major special responsibilities relating to the management of the Stability Pact for South-Eastern Europe.

Chapter 12

Concluding Remarks

Erik Pierre

I am going to address here a couple of general issues in international relations that I have encountered during my experiences as a diplomat. Between 1989 and 1992 I was the Deputy and Acting Head of the Swedish Mission to the OSCE in Vienna, Ambassador-at-Large for OSCE matters when Sweden was in the Chair of OSCE and Swedish Ambassador to Bosnia and Herzegovina.

At the end of my term in Vienna we started within the OSCE to address the issues of preventive diplomacy. In the early 1990s, the member States of the OSCE were facing totally new problems. Up to that point the organisation had successfully dealt with developing confidence-building measures. The OSCE had also, within its framework, brought a major breakthrough with its CFE (Conventional Armed Forces in Europe) Treaty as a basis for actual disarmament in Europe. Suddenly the Berlin Wall fell, the Warsaw Pact was dissolved and the Soviet Union went the same way. Up to then, the OSCE had dealt with avoiding conflicts between States which were basically playing according to the rules. The new challenges were more complicated with conflicts and open armed hostilities within States. Even with a superficial glance over the OSCE area of over fifty States, you could easily find dozens of conflicts or potential conflicts, which in one way or another had to be addressed.

In this new atmosphere the concept of preventive diplomacy emerged. It became quickly a concept *à la mode*. The OSCE was not prepared to do more than handle low-level conflicts and potential conflicts. Finally, after very difficult negotiations, the OSCE was able to send a Mission to Serbia in summer 1992 to monitor the situation in Vojvodina, Sandzak and Kosovo. It was a bold and timely move, in line with the new concept of 'preventive diplomacy'. It was also a CSCE Mission, and constantly had to handle various actions from the Yugoslav authorities. After almost one year the Mission was forced to leave. It is a good example of how rogue States undermine international efforts to address serious frictions which are threatening peace. However, in several cases of low-level friction, preventive diplomacy has more or less worked.

Preventive diplomacy might work when applied within a State where there is a certain amount of willingness to co-operate. When one of the parties inside a State is adamantly opposed to outside interference, it will be much more difficult to have any success with preventive diplomacy. Traditional preventive diplomacy easily reaches a stage where the contradictions are too strong to have a successful outcome.

Other preventive tools might be used, like economic, political and military measures, in order to defuse a political conflict. Between these and clusters of preventive diplomacy, there are clusters of other mid-term measures which, if intelligently applied, could be of great importance in order to mellow potential conflicts. Like, for instance, the Missions deployed by the OSCE in the Baltic States.

Within the framework of the discussed measures, the OSCE is an organisation which is growing more and more able to deal with these issues. The real problem of security occurs when the international community is faced with serious conflicts within rogue States or when such States are involved in one way or the other.

The dissolution of Yugoslavia falls into that category. We saw how the international community was more or less paralysed in dealing with this event and consequently unable to address the issues, basically because of a fundamental disagreement between the major powers within the EU and between the EU and the United States. We saw, for instance, how the United States supported the unity of Yugoslavia up to the end of 1991. Germany and Austria were of the view that the Yugoslav leaders were not able to run the country and that dissolution was inevitable and had reached the point of no return. France and the UK were of the view that it was not possible to keep the country together, and at the same time reluctantly agreed to recognise Slovenia and Croatia. In 1992, the position of the United States changed, but we still saw, from time to time in the following years, serious frictions between the United States on one side and the UK and France on the other. Most of these disputes took place inside the Contact Group (the USA, the UK, France, Germany, Russia and lately Italy). Only after the massacre in Srebrenica did a unified policy emerge in the summer of 1995.

One hears from time to time, that it was totally wrong to recognise Croatia. A French gentleman was tasked by the international community to head a commission to evaluate which of the republics were applicable for recognition. According to Badinter's report, Croatia could be recognised provided that the Constitution was changed in such a way that more rights were given to the minorities. Unfortunately such changes were not requested before Croatia was recognised. At the time, one major concern was that an international Presence on the ground to defuse the situation could not be established without the consent of the regime in Belgrade.

During the summer and autumn of 1991 the international community took extensive measures with the aim of stopping the war. Fourteen ceasefire agreements were signed. Those actions were too limited and quite often came too late. There was no preventive diplomacy: it was pure reactive diplomacy.

Having closely followed how the international community dealt with internal disputes and rogue regimes, it was even more frustrating to watch how the international community failed to implement its agreements in Bosnia and

Herzegovina. Four years after the signing of the Dayton Agreement, it is disturbing to note that several basic issues in the treaty have still not been implemented:

- the return of refugees is still unresolved;
- basic personal security for minorities is still at a far from acceptable level;
- the power of the national parties is basically unchanged;
- the informal political and economic power structures – public companies, intelligence services and security organs – are intact within the three competing national groups;
- consequently, the control of employment is in the hands of the informal power structures;
- the national parties are in essence opposed to key elements in the Dayton Agreement and they work to various degrees against the implementation of these elements.

I would like to focus for a moment on the economic structure dominated by publicly-owned enterprises, which are run by each informal power centre. It means there is still a totally politicised society, where economic considerations play a secondary role. It means also that the power centres control the employment situation down to those who will get a job or not. Since the informal power centres also control the security organs (including the intelligence-gathering system), the citizen feels constrained to subdued behaviour. In addition, these informal power centres are constantly undermining the implementation of the Dayton Agreement.

The Office of the High Representative has gradually been given more power to pave the way for implementation of the Dayton Agreement. Sometimes these new powers are referred to as the 'Bonn Powers'. Recently the OHR has started to dismiss central and local officials who openly undermined the implementation of the peace agreement. This is a very welcome move. Unfortunately, one can see how the local power players are circumventing these dismissals. Let me quote from an ESI draft paper 'Reshaping International Priorities in Bosnia and Herzegovina: Part Two – International Powers'.[1] In the first moves to dismiss local officials, the Deputy Mayor of Drvar Drago Tokmadzija in the northern part of the province of Herzegovina was forced to leave in April 1998:

> In Drvar, Drago Tokmacije has confirmed to be the most important local power broker. Since April 1998 he has been sacked on the further occasions: in February 1999 from holding any HDZ party post and in November 1999 from the Cantonal Privatisation Agency. He is still a prominent member of the management Board of the public company Finvest, the major employer in the area and a close associate of the senior HDZ leadership. In 1999 he publicly beat up a representative of a private company who had come to Drvar from Sarajevo to prepare the ground for an EC-funded infrastructure project. In spite of all this, because he continues to be influential, international officials working in Drvar continued to negotiate with him on

---

[1] This paper can be downloaded from the ESI website: www.esiweb.org.

local issues, not least the problem of organised violence against minority return, long after his dismissal.

Similar stories can be told for a large proportion of the 40 dismissed officials.

The Mayor of Bugojno is another notorious saboteur of all efforts for reconciliation after the war between Bosniacs and Croats. Many in Bosnia and abroad were relieved to see him dismissed, until it was learned that he continues undermining the peace process through the new Mayor.

Let me make a couple of more observations. There is a tendency within the international community to arrange elections in newly established countries without having the basic conditions available for free and fair elections. The elections in Bosnia and Herzegovina in 1996 are a good example. In the Dayton Agreement it was said that free and fair elections should be held during 1996 provided that the OSCE had found that the right conditions prevailed.

The Chairman of the OSCE at the time was the Foreign Minister of Switzerland, who presented a set of reasonable conditions which had to be met before he was prepared to give his consent. He, however, came under enormous pressure from the Great Powers and leading officials of the international community to say 'yes' even though these conditions were not met. When he finally declared that the election could be held, he elegantly implied that he was expressing a strong wish from most countries, which was not necessarily shared by him. It was a low point in the history of the OSCE.

Outside the set of conditions outlined by the Swiss Foreign Minister, there were other concerns. The United States wanted the elections, as a reason for US troops being able to leave. Other leading countries were of the view that a postponed election would have delayed the establishing of common institutions in Bosnia and Herzegovina, as called for in the Dayton Accords. The latter aspect was also the major reason for Carl Bildt, then the High Representative for Bosnia and Herzegovina, to press for the elections as planned.

It seems that the international community still has a tendency to justify its efforts by arranging elections. It seems that the mistake which was made in Bosnia and Herzegovina in 1996, is being repeated in Kosovo. One gets the impression that we, the Western countries, have a tendency to pave the way for undemocratic forces through democratic elections.

Finally, I would like to say a few things about the Stability Pact. It is a good initiative, but unfortunately there seems to be a division in attitude among the key players as to whether this Pact will be successful or not. The funding of the initiative is so far limited. At present, the major stumbling block in creating a viable Stability Pact for the Balkans is a non-participating Serbia. As long as Serbia is not part of the Stability Pact for the Balkans, it will be difficult to predict the outcome. That does not mean that the present work will be done in vain. There is a good chance to build a foundation for a Stability Pact, but there are still serious problems, which have to be solved in one way or another before such a foundation will be seen as a solid one.

It is, however, difficult to be optimistic about the near future. There are still dark clouds on the horizon. It is hard not to see similarities between the present development in Montenegro and the events in Bosnia and Herzegovina in late 1991 and early 1992. At the same time one cannot avoid seeing serious obstacles to development in Kosovo. The present strength of the UCK is particularly frightening, when it comes to the possibilities to create a democratic society. UCK seems to have such a firm grip over the local population that the non-supporters will be forced to give their tacit consent and the chance for other political forces to play a role are diminishing day after day. Any movement towards extended self-government or independence in Kosovo will create repercussions in Macedonia.

Macedonia has so far been lucky and skilful in avoiding an internal war between the two national groups. But one should not forget that the present cohesion in Macedonia is very fragile. Any Albanian nationalistic movement in Kosovo might easily spill over into Macedonia. We will be doing ourselves a serious disservice if we do not pay attention to the fragile political structure in Macedonia, and therefore the international community has to carefully handle the developments in Kosovo.

Chapter 13

Concluding Address

Louis Michel

In this chapter I would like to outline some considerations concerning the operational role of the OSCE in South-Eastern Europe.

The dialogue held for more than twenty-five years, before even the adoption of the Final Act of the Helsinki Conference, between all the States of the European continent has contributed much to the *rapprochement* confirmed by the symbolic act which was the destruction of the Berlin Wall.

The co-operation between the countries of Western Europe, of Central Europe and of Eastern Europe inaugurated at Helsinki should today concentrate its efforts on paying greater attention to those belonging to national minorities, the eternal victims of political and military struggles.

The humanitarian and democratic principles repeated and confirmed in the texts elaborated during the Conference on Security and Co-operation in Europe led to the creation of the Organisation for Security and Co-operation in Europe. This young institution has already seen in recent years the multiplication of specific Missions, defined case by case to respond to common objectives: peace, security and co-operation.

The recent Istanbul Summit reminded us that the OSCE approach to security has two aspects. The organisation treats questions relative to arms control, but also develops preventive diplomacy activities. It elaborates confidence-building measures, assumes an active role in promoting human rights and democracy, organises and monitors elections, observes social and economic imbalances liable to provoke destabilising tensions, and it wants to play a role in trans-border environmental management.

The Istanbul Summit Declaration highlighted the extent of the problems which confront the OSCE. The first of these concerns should always be the lot of the civil populations, victims of armed conflicts. The Charter for European Security also adopted at Istanbul underlines correctly, that if the old divisions between groups of States belong happily to the past, new risks have emerged. It has become obvious that security threats can come from internal conflicts, as much as conflicts between States. International terrorism, aggressive extremism, organised crime and drug trafficking constitute growing menaces. The participating States of the OSCE have undertaken to fight together against these new risks. Indeed they cannot be tackled without concerted action. Since other international organisations have already seen themselves granted competencies in these domains it is pertinent to ensure a prior co-ordination of existing means before envisaging others. The Platform for Cooperative Security annexed to the Charter is a first response to this need.

But sub-regional co-operation equally constitutes an important element for security. The Stability pact for South-Eastern Europe, elaborated on the initiative of the European Union and placed under the auspices of the OSCE, will contribute efficiently to the assurance of stability in this region of Europe.

To assure the stability in the whole of the zone of participating States, in particular in South-Eastern Europe, the OSCE institutions should be reinforced. The Charter opportunely draws some guidelines to respond to this goal.

An element which appears essential to me is also a more precise definition of the framework of action for Missions deployed by the OSCE and their relations with other bodies of the organisation itself. The propositions formulated at Istanbul to improve the rapid deployment of the necessary means to respond to urgent situations are important assets which should be used to their best potential.

PART III
APPENDICES

Report to the Chairman-in-Office on the Development of the South-Eastern Europe Regional Dimension of the OSCE

Robert L. Barry

Since 1995 the OSCE has shifted from a norm-setting conference to a field-based organization with over a dozen missions or other representative offices with tasks such as conduct of elections, human rights monitoring, democratization, police training and supervision, and regional military stabilization. This shift is particularly evident in South-Eastern Europe, where the OSCE now maintains a presence in five countries with a combined field presence of more than 3,000 national and international staff.

While the mandate of each OSCE presence in South-Eastern Europe is unique, the problems and issues they face are similar. Consequently, the goal of the OSCE's regional dimension is to improve the organization's own ability to deal with regional problems, to encourage host country co-operation at a regional level, and to provide support for the Stability Pact for South-Eastern Europe. The aim is to achieve these goals in three ways:

- by strengthening cooperation among OSCE missions in pursuit of clearly defined goals, such as refugee return;
- by initiating regional projects, both to deal with transborder issues such as organized crime and to use best practices to deal with common problems which are not transborder in nature, such as judicial reform;
- by initiating or supporting projects endorsed by the Stability Pact itself, such as the OSCE-supported task force on gender issues and the OSCE proposal for a legislative clearing house and resource center in the region.

Throughout all these efforts we are conscious of the need to seek partners and coordinate with those outside of our organization. The regional dimension seeks to build on OSCE's comparative advantages in South-Eastern Europe by contributing rather than duplicating initiatives of others in the region. We are well aware of the need for the international community to adopt a coordinated approach to South-Eastern Europe. This awareness has guided our analysis and efforts to address some of the key issues throughout the region.

Analysis of Regional Issues

The Sarajevo Summit demonstrated that there is considerable ambivalence towards the concept of regionalism among the countries of South-Eastern Europe. Many states of the region still view the process of integration into broader Euro-Atlantic political and economic structures from the perspective of competition rather than collaboration.

At the same time, the Sarajevo Summit also demonstrated that regional problems can be more readily resolved in a cooperative context. For example, inter-entity disputes within Bosnia and Herzegovina became less intractable when placed within the broader context of regional integration.

Key Regional Issues

As part of its regional initiative, the OSCE has launched a number of efforts to address regional problems within and outside the Stability Pact arena. Initially, these efforts are being supported through the resources of OSCE field missions, but soon the OSCE will have to mobilize resources from donors or turn over project management to other institutions.

Democracy and Human Rights

Refugee return is a top priority which involves all three working tables, and OSCE missions must work across borders and with UNHCR and other international partners to co-ordinate efforts and ensure information flows. The systematized co-operation being developed between the OSCE missions in Croatia and Bosnia and Herzegovina could serve as a model for dealing with this issue on a regional basis.

The status of women across the region has declined sharply over the past decade, with women experiencing growing discrimination in politics, employment and legal rights. The OSCE welcomed the lead role on gender issues given to it by the Stability Pact Working Table I on Human Rights and Democratization. The OSCE has launched a task force on gender issues, which will focus initially on increasing the participation of women in politics. The task force was inaugurated in Sarajevo in early November.

Indigenous human rights organizations, such as the Ombudsman are encountering obstacles in their efforts to maintain their independence and gain acceptance of their decisions. One step which will strengthen these regional organizations is an effort by the OSCE and the Council of Europe to support the ombudsman institutions throughout the region through the establishment of a regional network of ombudsmen.

Political parties continue to manipulate the electoral process. More must be done to professionalize election administration and empower civil society NGOs to observe and monitor elections. OSCE missions are working towards the creation of a regional association of election officials, and will continue to train local NGOs in election monitoring.

Strengthening independent media is also a key regional priority, and the OSCE should support efforts made under the Stability Pact Working Table I to promote freedom of the media throughout the region. All our endeavors must give a higher priority to the protection of journalists from terrorist attacks or politically motivated prosecutions. The OSCE will continue to undertake media development efforts in South-Eastern Europe, in recognition of the media's role as a key component of civil society and as an essential element in the system of checks and balances in the societies of the region.

Within the framework of Stability Pact Working Table I, OSCE field missions should take a leading role in promoting compliance with international agreements on protection of minorities; the implementation of recommendations in Roma and Sinti people is especially urgent.

OSCE field missions have found legal aid to individuals or interest groups an effective way of pursuing human rights cases through the courts. If donors are willing to fund such efforts they could be expanded regionally as a means of defending individual rights and promoting judicial reform.

The OSCE Parliamentary Assembly in coordination with other regional parliamentary groups ought to develop efforts to build capacity among regional parliamentarians with particular emphasis on legislative oversight of government actions.

Economic Reconstruction, Development and Reconstruction

The lack of meaningful microeconomic reform is a major obstacle to private investment and economic growth in the region. Political parties are fighting bitterly to maintain and expand their control over the economy, and this trend must be reversed. The OSCE has a stake in economic reform, and can support efforts by the international financial institutions and others. The OSCE's large field staff can also be helpful in advocacy efforts and in working to ensure that laws are implemented.

Harmonization of laws in the human rights and economic spheres with European standards is essential for integration. The OSCE has proposed the establishment of a legislative clearinghouse in Skopje, where regional governments can seek assistance and draw on the resources of institutions such as the Council of Europe, the European Union, and the Organization for Economic Cooperation and Development.

Security Issues

Military Security. At the Sarajevo Summit, both Bosnia and Herzegovina and Croatia called for negotiations towards reducing military budgets and manpower across the region. The OSCE Chairman-in-Office's Personal Representative for Article IV, Annex 1B of Dayton has been asked to explore such negotiations on a sub-regional basis with Bosnia and Herzegovina, Croatia and the Federal Republic of Yugoslavia.

In response to the demand for more extensive military confidence-building measures – including increased transparency in military budgets – the OSCE has asked the Special Representative of the Chairman-in-Office to pursue these issues in the context of Article V, Annex 1B. The chair of the Stability Pact Working Table III subtable on military security will monitor and co-ordinate these discussions.

Justice and Home Affairs. Organized crime and corruption has been identified – at the Sarajevo Summit and elsewhere – as a paramount obstacle to political and economic reform and individual security. A number of initiatives have been launched, both bilaterally and multilaterally, to deal with this growing problem, but most remain underdeveloped, underfunded and overlapping. Within the region, there is a need for better contacts among law-enforcement officials and prosecutors. In Bosnia and Herzegovina, for example, police and prosecutors do not even discuss issues between the two entities. A central problem is that heads of organized criminal groups enjoy protection from nationalist politicians and the former intelligence agencies. A new enforcement initiative is needed, and the OSCE is working to form a pilot task force on the trafficking of women and children, patterned on the Baltic Sea Task Force on Organized Crime. If this approach works, it could be applied to other forms of crime as well.

Disaster relief and emergency planning presents an opportunity for regional cooperation. As a consequence of regional instability there is a frequent need to cooperate in dealing with emergency situations. The Russian Federation has made interesting proposals for cooperative efforts and these should be examined at the next meeting of Stability Pact Working Table III.

Recommendations

Organizational Issues

Expanding the regional dimension of the OSCE's field activities should be an organizational priority for 2000, both on its own merits and because it will contribute to the Stability Pact's success. This will require strong support from the new Chairman-in-Office, since busy field missions cannot be expected to vigorously pursue regional initiatives on their own. In pursuit of this goal, the CiO should appoint a special envoy or a personal representative for regional issues, preferably a senior official of the same nationality who unquestionably speaks for the CiO.

Heads of OSCE field missions need to take responsibility for promoting regional projects and improving cooperation with other missions. The OSCE's central institutions need to pay more attention to needs identified by field missions and by the states of the region and take this into consideration when setting their priorities. By doing so these institutions will participate more fully in the OSCE's transition to an operational, field-based organization. The Secretariat has a supporting role to play in this effort. If the incoming CiO appoints a special envoy or personal representative to deal with the regional dimension, a group in the Secretariat should become his or her support staff.

For the OSCE to build a regional dimension, dedicated financial resources will be required. A number of donors are prepared to make voluntary contributions to be earmarked for projects involving two or more countries of the region, and international organizations such as the European Union may do the same. But the OSCE itself should set aside a modest amount of its budget for regional activities, which would include support for the special envoy/personal representative.

While missions must operate in accordance with the mandate as agreed by the host country, OSCE assistance in implementing Stability Pact-related projects, either via an existing mission or central institution (such as ODIHR or the Parliamentary Assembly) should be welcomed by each host country.

Given the similarity of problems faced by each OSCE mission, there needs to be more information exchange among missions on issues of common concern. We should not only promote greater collaboration among missions, but enable missions to draw on lessons learned from past experience elsewhere. To this end, the OSCE Secretariat's capacity to provide information on the various OSCE initiatives must be improved, in order to ensure that this information is readily accessible to the missions and other central institutions.

The Stability Pact and OSCE Regional Projects

The Stability Pact itself presumes a central role for the OSCE, and the OSCE has offered its substantial field presence and mechanisms in support of Stability Pact goals. But the future of the relationship remains uncertain, and both the OSCE and the Stability Pact Coordinator need to do more to put it on a firm footing. Efforts by the Coordinator and the chairs of the Working Tables to draw OSCE field missions into their work would pay great dividends for both. Field missions should not wait to be invited, but should volunteer their assistance where needed. Lines of communication should also be strengthened to allow more input from field personnel on Stability Pact-related issues.

Perhaps the most powerful catalyst for reform is the nearly universal desire for integration into Europe. For this incentive to have real effect, however, the path to integration must be clearly marked and the institutions of Europe need to be sure the path is followed. All members of the international community, including the OSCE, must speak with a single voice on this issue. If the requirements for accession to these institutions are relaxed to accommodate countries which are unable or unwilling to reform, integration will not take place in any meaningful way and the Stability Pact will lose its relevance.

The OSCE and the Stability Pact need to keep the issue of regional ownership always before them. This includes, in particular, involving NGOs and other civil society representatives. Close attention must be paid to the wishes of the citizens of host countries.

There are a great many overlapping and under-funded regional initiatives launched by international organizations, individual countries and NGOs. The Stability Pact Coordinator and the Chairman-in-Office should lead an effort to merge and rationalize them. This will make coordination simpler and more effective.

The OSCE has launched a number of modest regional projects. These projects need to be results-oriented and consistently pursued. The OSCE cannot afford to have these initiatives wither because of inattention by mission management or lack of resources.

Both the Stability Pact and the OSCE must try harder to avoid allowing regional initiatives to deteriorate into 'talking shops'. While there is no doubt that periodic conferences and stock-taking exercises may be means to an end, they are not ends in themselves. Greater attention must therefore be paid to ensuring concrete follow-up on recommendations that do emerge from conferences and workshops.

Istanbul Summit Declaration, 19 November 1999

1. We, the Heads of State or Government of the participating States of the OSCE, have assembled in Istanbul on the eve of the twenty-first century and of the twenty-fifth anniversary of the Helsinki Final Act. Since we last met we have transformed the OSCE to meet unprecedented challenges. When we met in Lisbon, the first large-scale OSCE field operation had just been established, in Bosnia and Herzegovina. During the three intervening years, we have increased dramatically the number and size of our field operations. Our common institutions have grown in number and in the level of their activities. The OSCE has expanded the scale and substance of its efforts. This has greatly strengthened the OSCE's contribution to security and co-operation across the OSCE area. We pay special tribute to the women and men whose dedication and hard work have made the Organization's achievements possible.

2. Today, we adopted a Charter for European Security in order to strengthen security and stability in our region and improve the operational capabilities of our Organization. We task the OSCE Permanent Council to take the necessary decisions to implement promptly the new steps agreed upon in this Charter. We need the contribution of a strengthened OSCE to meet the risks and challenges facing the OSCE area, to improve human security and thereby to make a difference in the life of the individual, which is the aim of all our efforts. We reiterate unreservedly our commitment to respect human rights and fundamental freedoms and to abstain from any form of discrimination. We also reiterate our respect for international humanitarian law. We pledge our commitment to intensify efforts to prevent conflicts in the OSCE area, and when they occur to resolve them peacefully. We will work closely with other international organizations and institutions on the basis of the Platform for Co-operative Security, which we adopted as a part of our Charter.

3. The situation in Kosovo, FRY, in particular the humanitarian situation, remains a major challenge for the OSCE. Our thoughts still go out to the large number of Kosovo Albanians and others who lost their lives, those who saw their property destroyed and the hundreds of thousands who were expelled from and abandoned their homes. Now most of these refugees have returned. As the difficult work of rehabilitation advances, remaining refugees will be able to return. The OSCE Mission in Kosovo forms an essential part of the broader United Nations Mission

working under United Nations Security Council Resolution 1244. The OSCE Mission today has more than 1,400 staff members, and plays a vital role in the process of rebuilding a multi-ethnic society in Kosovo; the first class from the OSCE Police School has graduated, and the OSCE training of judicial and administrative personnel has started. The Organization assists in developing a civil society, in supporting the formation of a pluralistic political party landscape, free media and a viable NGO community. The OSCE plays a leading role in promoting and protecting human rights, and establishing respect for the rule of law. The success of this work is essential if democracy is to take root. We pledge to give it our full support. As we advance in these areas, we accelerate our work towards creating the necessary conditions for the first free elections in Kosovo, which the OSCE has been tasked to organize. We will seek to involve the local population increasingly in the efforts of the OSCE Mission.

4. Against the background of years of repression, intolerance and violence in Kosovo, the challenge is to build a multi-ethnic society on the basis of substantial autonomy respecting the sovereignty and territorial integrity of the Federal Republic of Yugoslavia, pending final settlement in accordance with UNSCR 1244. We expect this Resolution to be fully implemented and strictly adhered to by all concerned. We will assist all inhabitants of Kosovo. But they, and those who aspire to be their leaders, must work together towards a multi-ethnic society where the rights of each citizen are fully and equally respected. They must fight decisively against the cycle of hate and revenge and bring about reconciliation among all ethnic groups. Over the recent months, we have witnessed a new exodus from Kosovo, this time of Serbs and other non-Albanians. The necessary conditions must be restored so that those who have fled recently can return and enjoy their rights. Those who fought and suffered for their rights must now stand up for the equal rights of others. We firmly reject any further violence and any form of ethnic discrimination. Failure to oppose such acts will affect the security of the region.

5. The democratic shortcomings in the Federal Republic of Yugoslavia remain one of the fundamental sources of grave concern in the region. The leaders and people of the Federal Republic of Yugoslavia must put the country firmly on the path towards democracy and respect for human rights and fundamental freedoms. When conditions permit, the OSCE stands ready to assist in order to accelerate democratization, promote independent media and hold free and fair elections in the Federal Republic of Yugoslavia. We emphasize our desire to see the Federal Republic of Yugoslavia as a full partner. Real progress towards democracy will be a positive step towards equal participation of the Federal Republic of Yugoslavia in the international community, including in the OSCE, and will create a new basis for growth and prosperity.

6. We remain committed to a democratic, multi-ethnic Bosnia and Herzegovina based on the General Framework Agreement for Peace. We underline the importance of improving the functioning of common institutions, and of the continued assumption by those and other institutions of tasks undertaken by the international community. We expect Bosnia and Herzegovina to rapidly adopt the permanent election law, so that it can be implemented prior to the general elections scheduled for the autumn of 2000. We appeal to all the leaders of Bosnia and Herzegovina to take decisive steps towards bringing its two entities closer together and to create a situation where persons, goods and services can circulate freely within a single State to the benefit of stability and prosperity. We underline the importance of respect for the rule of law and of vigorous efforts to fight organized crime and corruption, which constitute a great threat to economic reform and prosperity. We remain committed to the return of refugees and internally displaced persons, in particular minority returns.

7. We underscore the importance of working with Croatian authorities to intensify efforts towards reconciliation in Croatia. The OSCE pledges to continue its assistance to a multi-ethnic Croatia through post-war confidence-building and reconciliation. We look forward to faster progress towards the return of refugees and displaced persons and the implementation of relevant international standards, particularly those related to equal treatment without regard to ethnicity, freedom of the media, and free and fair elections. The OSCE's police monitoring in the Danubian region of Croatia, which has played a valuable role in protecting the rights of individuals, demonstrates the OSCE's ability to develop new operational capabilities quickly and efficiently.

8. We reaffirm our commitment to assist Albania as it continues its social, political and economic reform process following the setbacks caused by the upheaval of 1997 and the Kosovo refugee crisis of 1999. Noting the recent progress, we call upon the Government and all political parties to improve the political atmosphere, thereby strengthening democratic institutions. We encourage the new Government of Albania to continue its fight against crime and corruption. The OSCE is committed to continue its assistance and to work closely with the European Union and international organizations within the framework of the 'Friends of Albania'.

9. We commend the Government of the former Yugoslav Republic of Macedonia for its commitment to domestic reforms designed to enhance stability and economic prosperity. We reaffirm the OSCE's determination to support its efforts in this process, and emphasize the importance of continued attention to the development of inter-ethnic relations.

10. We pay tribute to the Governments and peoples of Albania and the former Yugoslav Republic of Macedonia, as most affected countries, as well as those of other neighbouring countries for their hospitality during the Kosovo refugee crisis

and for their generosity in shouldering a heavy political and economic burden during this period.

11. Our experiences in South Eastern Europe demonstrate the need for a broader view of the region. We therefore welcome the adoption by the Cologne Ministerial Conference on 10 June 1999 of the Stability Pact for South-Eastern Europe, launched on the initiative of the European Union, which plays a leading role in co-operation with other participating and facilitating States, international organizations and institutions. We reinforce the message from the Sarajevo Summit: regional co-operation will serve as a catalyst for the integration of countries in the region into broader structures. The OSCE, under whose auspices the Stability Pact is placed, has a key role to play in contributing to its success, and we task the Permanent Council to develop a regional strategy to support its aims. We welcome the reports provided to us by the Special Co-ordinator for the Stability Pact and the Special Envoy of the OSCE Chairman-in-Office. The OSCE will work in close concert with our participating States and with non-governmental organizations in the region.

12. We consider that the work of the International Criminal Tribunal for the former Yugoslavia is crucial to achieving lasting peace and justice in the region, and reiterate the obligation of all to co-operate fully with the Tribunal.

13. During this year we have witnessed a significant increase in our co-operation with the five participating States in Central Asia. Political dialogue has gained from a growing number of high-level visits from the Central Asian States to the OSCE and by OSCE representatives to Central Asia. With the continuing support of our partners in Central Asia, the OSCE has now established offices in all five States. This in particular has contributed to an expansion of our co-operative activities in all OSCE dimensions. Reiterating our target of achieving comprehensive security throughout the OSCE area, we strongly welcome these positive developments. We are convinced that necessary progress in the difficult and complex transition process will be stimulated by an increase in our efforts based on co-operation and our common commitments. Strengthening the rule of law, the respect for human rights and fundamental freedoms as well as the development of civil societies constitute one of the centrepieces in our broad framework of co-operative efforts. In this regard, we welcome the process of signing of Memoranda of Understanding between the ODIHR and the Central Asian participating States.

14. We share the concerns expressed by the participating States in Central Asia regarding international terrorism, violent extremism, organized crime and drug and arms trafficking. We agree that national, regional and joint action by the international community is necessary to cope with these threats, including those stemming from areas neighbouring the OSCE participating States. We further

recognize the importance of addressing economic and environmental risks in the region, such as issues related to water resources, energy and erosion. We are convinced that strengthening regional co-operation will promote stability and security in Central Asia, and we welcome the active approach taken by the Chairman-in-Office to this effect.

15. Reaffirming our strong support for the sovereignty and territorial integrity of Georgia, we stress the need for solving the conflicts with regard to the Tskhinvali region/South Ossetia and Abkhazia, Georgia, particularly by defining the political status of these regions within Georgia. Respect for human rights and development of joint democratic institutions as well as the prompt, safe and unconditional return of refugees and internally displaced persons will contribute to peaceful settlement of these conflicts. We underscore the importance of taking concrete steps in this direction. We welcome progress reached at this Summit Meeting in the Georgian–Russian negotiations on the reduction of Russian military equipment in Georgia.

16. With regard to the Tskhinvali region/South Ossetia, Georgia, some progress has been made towards solving the conflict. We emphasize the importance of maintaining and intensifying the dialogue which is now under way. In light of further progress, we believe that an early meeting in Vienna, with participation of experts from this region, should be used to take decisive steps towards a solution. The establishment by the parties concerned of a legal framework for refugee and internally displaced persons housing and property restitution will facilitate the early return of refugees and internally displaced persons to the region. We also urge the early signing of the Georgian–Russian economic rehabilitation agreement and encourage further international economic assistance.

17. We continue to support the leading role of the United Nations in Abkhazia, Georgia. We emphasize the importance of breaking the current deadlock with regard to finding a peaceful solution to the conflict. In this respect we – and in particular those of us who belong to the Friends of the United Nations Secretary-General – are ready to work with the United Nations to prepare and submit a draft document addressing the distribution of constitutional competencies between the central authorities of Georgia and authorities of Abkhazia, Georgia. We reiterate our strong condemnation as formulated in the Budapest and Lisbon Summit Documents, of the 'ethnic cleansing' resulting in mass destruction and forcible expulsion of predominantly Georgian population in Abkhazia, Georgia, and of the violent acts in May 1998 in the Gali region. In light of the precarious situation of the returnees, we recommend that a fact-finding mission with the participation of the OSCE and the United Nations be dispatched early next year to the Gali region to assess, inter alia, reported cases of continued 'ethnic cleansing'. Such a mission would provide a basis for increased international support for the unconditional and safe return of refugees and internally displaced persons and contribute to the

general stability in the area. We consider the so-called presidential elections and referendum in Abkhazia, Georgia, this year as unacceptable and illegitimate.

18. We welcome the encouraging steps which have been recently taken in the process of the settlement of the Trans-Dniestrian problem. The Summit in Kiev (July 1999) became an important event in this regard. However, there have been no tangible shifts on the major issue – defining the status of the Trans-Dniestrian region. We reaffirm that in the resolution of this problem the sovereignty and territorial integrity of the Republic of Moldova should be ensured. We stand for the continuation and deployment of the negotiation process and call on all sides and in particular the Trans-Dniestrian authorities to demonstrate the political will required to negotiate a peaceful and early elimination of the consequences of the conflict. We appreciate the continuation of the mediating efforts of the Russian Federation, Ukraine and the OSCE in the negotiation process on the future status of the Trans-Dniestrian region within the Republic of Moldova. We take note of the positive role of the joint peacekeeping forces in securing stability in the region.

19. Recalling the decisions of the Budapest and Lisbon Summits and Oslo Ministerial Meeting, we reiterate our expectation of an early, orderly and complete withdrawal of Russian troops from Moldova. In this context, we welcome the recent progress achieved in the removal and destruction of the Russian military equipment stockpiled in the Trans-Dniestrian region of Moldova and the completion of the destruction of non-transportable ammunition.

We welcome the commitment by the Russian Federation to complete withdrawal of the Russian forces from the territory of Moldova by the end of 2002. We also welcome the willingness of the Republic of Moldova and of the OSCE to facilitate this process, within their respective abilities, by the agreed deadline.

We recall that an international assessment mission is ready to be dispatched without delay to explore removal and destruction of Russian ammunition and armaments. With the purpose of securing the process of withdrawal and destruction, we will instruct the Permanent Council to consider the expansion of the mandate of the OSCE Mission to Moldova in terms of ensuring transparency of this process and co-ordination of financial and technical assistance offered to facilitate withdrawal and destruction. Furthermore, we agree to consider the establishment of a fund for voluntary international financial assistance to be administered by the OSCE.

20. We received the report of the Co-Chairmen of the OSCE Minsk Group on the evolving situation and recent developments connected with the Nagorno-Karabakh conflict and commend their efforts. We applaud in particular the intensified dialogue between the Presidents of Armenia and Azerbaijan, whose regular contacts have created opportunities to dynamize the process of finding a lasting and comprehensive solution to the problem. We firmly support this dialogue and encourage its continuation, with the hope of resuming negotiations within the

OSCE Minsk Group. We also confirm that the OSCE and its Minsk Group, which remains the most appropriate format for finding a solution, stand ready to further advance the peace process and its future implementation, including by providing all necessary assistance to the parties.

21. We welcome the opening of an OSCE Office in Yerevan this year and the decision to open a similar office in Baku. These steps will enable the OSCE to strengthen our co-operation with Armenia and Azerbaijan.

22. We strongly support the work of the Advisory and Monitoring Group in Belarus, which has worked closely with the Belarusian authorities as well as with opposition parties and leaders and NGOs in promoting democratic institutions and compliance with OSCE commitments, thus facilitating a resolution of the constitutional controversy in Belarus. We emphasize that only a real political dialogue in Belarus can pave the way for free and democratic elections through which the foundations for real democracy can be developed. We would welcome early progress in this political dialogue with the OSCE participation, in close co-operation with the OSCE Parliamentary Assembly. We stress the necessity of removing all remaining obstacles to this dialogue by respecting the principles of the rule of law and the freedom of the media.

23. In connection with the recent chain of events in North Caucasus, we strongly reaffirm that we fully acknowledge the territorial integrity of the Russian Federation and condemn terrorism in all its forms. We underscore the need to respect OSCE norms. We agree that in light of the humanitarian situation in the region it is important to alleviate the hardships of the civilian population, including by creating appropriate conditions for international organizations to provide humanitarian aid. We agree that a political solution is essential, and that the assistance of the OSCE would contribute to achieving that goal. We welcome the willingness of the OSCE to assist in the renewal of a political dialogue. We welcome the agreement of the Russian Federation to a visit by the Chairman-in-Office to the region. We reaffirm the existing mandate of the OSCE Assistance Group in Chechnya. In this regard, we also welcome the willingness of the Russian Federation to facilitate these steps, which will contribute to creating conditions for stability, security, and economic prosperity in the region.

24. In a year which has seen the deployment of our largest ever mission, we have been able to welcome the successful conclusion of the work of one of our smallest, the OSCE Representative to the Joint Committee on the Skrunda Radar Station. We congratulate the parties involved in decommissioning the Radar Station on their efforts, undertaken in a spirit of constructive co-operation.

25. We welcome the successful completion of the work of the OSCE Mission to Ukraine. This work has been an important contribution by the OSCE to the process

of stabilization in its Autonomous Republic of Crimea. We look forward to continued co-operation between Ukraine and the OSCE, including through the OSCE Project Co-ordinator in Ukraine, on the basis of its mandate and the Memorandum of Understanding.

26. With a large number of elections ahead of us, we are committed to these being free and fair, and in accordance with OSCE principles and commitments. This is the only way in which there can be a stable basis for democratic development. We appreciate the role of the ODIHR in assisting countries to develop electoral legislation in keeping with OSCE principles and commitments, and we agree to follow up promptly ODIHR's election assessments and recommendations. We value the work of the ODIHR and the OSCE Parliamentary Assembly – before, during and after elections – which further contributes to the democratic process. We are committed to secure the full right of persons belonging to minorities to vote and to facilitate the right of refugees to participate in elections held in their countries of origin. We pledge to ensure fair competition among candidates as well as parties, including through their access to the media and respect for the right of assembly.

27. We commit ourselves to ensuring the freedom of the media as a basic condition for pluralistic and democratic societies. We are deeply concerned about the exploitation of media in areas of conflict to foment hatred and ethnic tension and the use of legal restrictions and harassment to deprive citizens of free media. We underline the need to secure freedom of expression, which is an essential element of political discourse in any democracy. We support the Office of the Representative on Freedom of the Media in its efforts to promote free and independent media.

28. In the year of the 10th anniversary of the adoption of the Convention on the Rights of the Child, and putting the OSCE's Copenhagen commitments into practice, we commit ourselves to actively promote children's rights and interests, especially in conflict and post-conflict situations. We will regularly address the rights of children in the work of the OSCE, including by organizing a special meeting dedicated to children in armed conflict during the year 2000. We will pay particular attention to the physical and psychological well-being of children involved in or affected by armed conflict.

29. The Co-ordinator of OSCE Economic and Environmental Activities should, under the authority of the Chairman-in-Office and the Secretary General and in close co-operation with the relevant OSCE field operations, develop regular reports concerning economic and environmental risks to security. These reports should include questions of promoting public awareness of the relationship between economic and environmental problems and security and the relationship between our Organization and others concerned with the promotion of economic

and environmental security within the OSCE area. Such reports will be discussed by the Permanent Council.

30. We reaffirm our commitment to ensure that laws and policies fully respect the rights of persons belonging to national minorities, in particular in relation to issues affecting cultural identity. Specifically, we emphasize the requirement that laws and policies regarding the educational, linguistic and participatory rights of persons belonging to national minorities conform to applicable international standards and conventions. We also support the adoption and full implementation of comprehensive anti-discrimination legislation to promote full equality of opportunities for all. We commend the essential work of the High Commissioner on National Minorities. We reaffirm that we will increase our efforts to implement the recommendations of the High Commissioner on National Minorities.

31. We deplore violence and other manifestations of racism and discrimination against minorities, including the Roma and Sinti. We commit ourselves to ensure that laws and policies fully respect the rights of Roma and Sinti and, where necessary, to promote anti-discrimination legislation to this effect. We underline the importance of careful attention to the problems of the social exclusion of Roma and Sinti. These issues are primarily a responsibility of the participating States concerned. We emphasize the important role that the ODIHR Contact Point for Roma and Sinti issues can play in providing support. A further helpful step might be the elaboration by the Contact Point of an action plan of targeted activities, drawn up in co-operation with the High Commissioner on National Minorities and others active in this field, notably the Council of Europe.

32. In line with our commitment to ensure full equality between women and men, we look forward to an early approval and implementation of an OSCE gender action plan.

33. In the framework of our commitment to further strengthening of the operational capacities of the OSCE Secretariat, we will improve the OSCE employment conditions so that it can better compete for and retain well qualified personnel to enable the Secretariat to carry out its tasks and fulfil its other responsibilities. We will take into account the need for geographic diversity and gender balance when recruiting personnel to OSCE institutions and field operations.

34. We note that a large number of participating States have not been able to implement the 1993 Rome Ministerial Council decision on legal capacity of the OSCE institutions and on privileges and immunities. With a view to improve this situation, a determined effort should be made to review issues related to the implementation of commitments under the 1993 Rome Ministerial decision. To this end, we task the Permanent Council, through an informal open-ended working

group to draw up a report to the next Ministerial Council Meeting, including recommendations on how to improve the situation.

35. To address the challenges in the OSCE area quickly and efficiently new instruments are required. We welcome the establishment, in the Charter, of a Rapid Expert Assistance and Co-operation Teams (REACT) programme for the OSCE. We commit ourselves to make this concept fully operational at the shortest possible time. We are determined as a matter of priority to implement the decision made in the Charter. We will provide the expertise required and commit the necessary resources according to established procedures. We take note of the letter from the Secretary General to the Permanent Council concerning the rapid deployment of expertise. We request the Permanent Council and the Secretary General to establish a task force within the Conflict Prevention Centre aimed at developing the REACT programme and a budget that will enable REACT to be fully operational by 30 June 2000.

36. We task the Permanent Council and the Secretary General to implement within the same time frame, our decision in the Charter to set up an Operation Centre within the Conflict Prevention Centre, with a small core staff having expertise relevant for all kinds of OSCE operations, which can be expanded rapidly when required, and the decisions made to strengthen the Secretariat and our field operations.

37. We have in the Charter reaffirmed our commitment to the rule of law and stressed the need to combat corruption. We task the Permanent Council to examine how best to contribute to efforts to combat corruption, taking into account efforts of other organizations such as the Organization for Economic Co-operation and Development, Council of Europe and the United Nations. The results of this work will be reported to the 2000 Ministerial Meeting.

38. The fact that we are meeting in Turkey, which only recently suffered terrible earthquakes, brings home to us the major impact of natural disasters. We need to strengthen the international community's ability to respond to such events, by improving the co-ordination of the efforts of participating States, international organizations and NGOs. We task the Permanent Council to discuss this matter further.

39. We welcome the successful adaptation of the Treaty on Conventional Armed Forces in Europe. The adapted Treaty will provide a greater degree of military stability through a stricter system of limitations, increased transparency and lower levels of conventional armed forces in its area of application. We hope the States Parties will move forward expeditiously to facilitate completion of national ratification procedures, taking into account their common commitment to, and the central importance of, full and continued implementation of the Treaty and its

associated documents until and following entry into force of the Agreement on Adaptation. Upon entry into force of the Agreement on Adaptation, OSCE participating States with territory in the area between the Atlantic Ocean and the Ural Mountains may apply for accession to the adapted Treaty, thereby providing an important additional contribution to European stability and security.

40. We welcome the OSCE Forum for Security Co-operation's efforts to advance security dialogue, co-operation, transparency and mutual confidence, as well as its work on the OSCE concept of comprehensive and indivisible security in accordance with its mandate of Helsinki 1992. We welcome the conclusion of the review process resulting in the adoption of the Vienna Document 1999 on confidence- and security-building measures, a key element of politico-military co-operation and stability. It improves current CSBMs and emphasizes the importance of regional co-operation. We remain fully committed to the principles contained in the Code of Conduct on politico-military aspects of security. We welcome the decision of the FSC to launch a broad and comprehensive discussion on all aspects of the problem of the spread of small arms and light weapons and to study concrete measures to deal with this issue, in order to respond to the challenge to peace and stability stemming from the excessive and destabilizing accumulation and uncontrolled spread of these weapons.

41. We note with satisfaction that the negotiations on regional stability, as foreseen under Article V of Annex 1-B of the General Framework Agreement for Peace, have entered their substantive phase. A successful outcome to the on-going Article V negotiations would make a significant contribution to security and stability in the region. We urge the states participating in the Article V negotiations to aim to conclude their work by the end of 2000. We appreciate the OSCE's active role in facilitating the implementation of the Agreement on Confidence- and Security-Building Measures in Bosnia and Herzegovina and the Agreement on Sub-Regional Arms Control negotiated under Annex 1-B of the General Framework Agreement for Peace in Bosnia and Herzegovina.

42. We reaffirm the significance of the Open Skies Treaty: in this respect, convinced that trial flights are in no way a substitute for the regime of observation flights as set forth in the Treaty, we urge early completion of the process of its ratification and entry into force.

43. We note the widespread human suffering caused by anti-personnel mines and note the entry into force on 1 March 1999 of the Convention on the Prohibition of the Use, Stockpiling, Production and Transfer of Anti-Personnel Mines and on their Destruction. We also note the entry into force on 3 December 1998 of the Amended Mines Protocol to the UN Convention on Prohibitions or Restrictions on the Use of Certain Conventional Weapons which may be deemed to be Excessively Injurious or to have Indiscriminate Effects. We reaffirm our support

for international co-operation in promoting global humanitarian action against anti-personnel mines, including promoting mine clearance activities, mine awareness programs, and the care, rehabilitation and social and economic reintegration of mine victims.

44. We take note of the report of the Chairman-in-Office on discussions held this year with regard to reviewing the scale and criteria for financing OSCE activities and instruct the Permanent Council to continue its discussions with a view to reaching agreement before the OSCE Ministerial Council Meeting in November/December 2000, so that this agreement can be applied after 31 December 2000, in accordance with the decision taken at the 1997 Copenhagen Ministerial Council Meeting.

45. We reconfirm the importance we attach to the relationship with our Partners for Co-operation as set out in the Charter for European Security. In light of our relationship with our Mediterranean Partners, Algeria, Egypt, Israel, Jordan, Morocco and Tunisia, we reaffirm that strengthening security and co-operation in the Mediterranean area is of major importance to the stability in the OSCE area. We therefore intend to enhance our dialogue and joint activities with them. We will furthermore strengthen our relationship with Japan and the Republic of Korea. We appreciate the contributions made by Japan to OSCE activities.

46. We express our gratitude to the High Commissioner on National Minorities, Mr. Max van der Stoel, for his willingness to continue in his position until a new High Commissioner on National Minorities has been appointed at the latest at the OSCE Ministerial Meeting in Vienna in November/December 2000.

47. The next Ministerial Council will take place in Vienna in November/December 2000, and will take a decision on the time and place of the next meeting of the Heads of State or Government of the OSCE participating States.

48. We welcome and accept the offer of Romania to exercise the function of Chairman-in-Office in 2001.

Charter for European Security
Istanbul, 19 November 1999

Organization for Security and Co-operation in Europe
Istanbul Summit, 19 November 1999

Charter for European Security

List of Contents

Introduction
I   Our Common Challenges
II Our Common Foundations
III Our Common Response
      Co-operation with Other Organizations: the Platform for Co-operative Security, Solidarity and Partnership
      Our Institutions
      The Human Dimension
      The Politico-Military Dimension
      The Economic and Environmental Dimension
      Rule of Law and Fight Against Corruption
IV Our Common Instruments
      Enhancing Our Dialogue
      OSCE Field Operations
      Rapid Response (REACT)
      Operation Center
      Police-Related Activities
      Peacekeeping
      The Court of Conciliation and Arbitration
V Our Partners for Co-operation
VI Conclusion

Operational Document – The Platform for Co-Operative Security

I. The Platform
II. Modalities for Co-operative Security

CHARTER FOR EUROPEAN SECURITY
Istanbul, November 1999

1. At the dawn of the twenty-first century we, the Heads of State or Government of the OSCE participating States, declare our firm commitment to a free, democratic and more integrated OSCE area where participating States are at peace with each other, and individuals and communities live in freedom, prosperity and security. To implement this commitment, we have decided to take a number of new steps. We have agreed to:

- Adopt the Platform for Co-operative Security, in order to strengthen co-operation between the OSCE and other international organizations and institutions, thereby making better use of the resources of the international community;
- Develop the OSCE's role in peacekeeping, thereby better reflecting the Organization's comprehensive approach to security;
- Create Rapid Expert Assistance and Co-operation Teams (REACT), thereby enabling the OSCE to respond quickly to demands for assistance and for large civilian field operations;
- Expand our ability to carry out police-related activities in order to assist in maintaining the primacy of law;
- Establish an Operation Centre, in order to plan and deploy OSCE field operations;
- Strengthen the consultation process within the OSCE by establishing the Preparatory Committee under the OSCE Permanent Council.

We are committed to preventing the outbreak of violent conflicts wherever possible. The steps we have agreed to take in this Charter will strengthen the OSCE's ability in this respect as well as its capacity to settle conflicts and to rehabilitate societies ravaged by war and destruction. The Charter will contribute to the formation of a common and indivisible security space. It will advance the creation of an OSCE area free of dividing lines and zones with different levels of security.

I. Our Common Challenges

2. The last decade of the twentieth century has brought great achievements in the OSCE area, co-operation has replaced previous confrontation, but the danger of conflicts between States has not been eliminated. We have put Europe's old divisions behind us, but new risks and challenges have emerged. Since we signed the Charter of Paris it has become more obvious that threats to our security can stem from conflicts within States as well as from conflicts between States. We

have experienced conflicts which have often resulted from flagrant violations of OSCE norms and principles. We have witnessed atrocities of a kind we had thought were relegated to the past. In this decade it has become clear that all such conflicts can represent a threat to the security of all OSCE participating States.

3. We are determined to learn from the dangers of confrontation and division between States as well as from tragedies of the last decade. Security and peace must be enhanced through an approach which combines two basic elements, we must build confidence among people within States and strengthen co-operation between States. Therefore, we will strengthen existing instruments and develop new ones to provide assistance and advice. We will reinforce our efforts to ensure full respect for human rights and fundamental freedoms, including the rights of persons belonging to national minorities. In parallel, we will strengthen our capacity to enhance confidence and security between States. We are determined to develop the means at our disposal to settle peacefully disputes between them.

4. International terrorism, violent extremism, organized crime and drug trafficking represent growing challenges to security. Whatever its motives, terrorism in all its forms and manifestations is unacceptable. We will enhance our efforts to prevent the preparation and financing of any act of terrorism on our territories and deny terrorists safe havens. The excessive and destabilizing accumulation and uncontrolled spread of small arms and light weapons represent a threat to peace and security. We are committed to strengthening our protection against these new risks and challenges; strong democratic institutions and the rule of law are the foundation for this protection. We are also determined to co-operate more actively and closely with each other to meet these challenges.

5. Acute economic problems and environmental degradation may have serious implications for our security. Co-operation in the fields of economy, science and technology and the environment will be of critical importance. We will strengthen our responses to such threats through continued economic and environmental reforms, by stable and transparent frameworks for economic activity and by promoting market economies, while paying due attention to economic and social rights. We applaud the unprecedented process of economic transformation taking place in many participating States. We encourage them to continue this reform process, which will contribute to security and prosperity in the entire OSCE area. We will step up our efforts across all dimensions of the OSCE to combat corruption and to promote the rule of law.

6. We confirm that security in areas nearby, in particular in the Mediterranean area as well as areas in direct proximity to participating States, such as those of Central Asia, is of increasing importance to the OSCE. We recognize that instability in these areas creates challenges that directly affect the security and prosperity of OSCE States.

II. Our Common Foundations

7. We reaffirm our full adherence to the Charter of the United Nations, and to the Helsinki Final Act, the Charter of Paris and all other OSCE documents to which we have agreed. These documents represent our common commitments and are the foundation for our work. They have helped us to bring about an end to the old confrontation in Europe and to foster a new era of democracy, peace and solidarity throughout the OSCE area. They established clear standards for participating States' treatment of each other and of all individuals within their territories. All OSCE commitments, without exception, apply equally to each participating State. Their implementation in good faith is essential for relations between States, between governments and their peoples, as well as between the organizations of which they are members. Participating States are accountable to their citizens and responsible to each other for their implementation of their OSCE commitments. We regard these commitments as our common achievement and therefore consider them to be matters of immediate and legitimate concern to all participating States.

We reaffirm the OSCE as a regional arrangement under Chapter VIII of the Charter of the United Nations and as a primary organization for the peaceful settlement of disputes within its region and as a key instrument for early warning, conflict prevention, crisis management and post-conflict rehabilitation. The OSCE is the inclusive and comprehensive organization for consultation, decision-making and co-operation in its region.

8. Each participating State has an equal right to security. We reaffirm the inherent right of each and every participating State to be free to choose or change its security arrangements, including treaties of alliance, as they evolve. Each State also has the right to neutrality. Each participating State will respect the rights of all others in these regards. They will not strengthen their security at the expense of the security of other States. Within the OSCE no State, group of States or organization can have any pre-eminent responsibility for maintaining peace and stability in the OSCE area or can consider any part of the OSCE area as its sphere of influence.

9. We will build our relations in conformity with the concept of common and comprehensive security, guided by equal partnership, solidarity and transparency. The security of each participating State is inseparably linked to that of all others. We will address the human, economic, political and military dimensions of security as an integral whole.

10. We will continue to uphold consensus as the basis for OSCE decision-making. The OSCE's flexibility and ability to respond quickly to a changing political environment should remain at the heart of the OSCE's co-operative and inclusive approach to common and indivisible security.

11. We recognize the primary responsibility of the United Nations Security Council for the maintenance of international peace and security and its crucial role in contributing to security and stability in our region. We reaffirm our rights and obligations under the Charter of the United Nations, including our commitment on the issue of the non-use of force or the threat of force. In this connection, we also reaffirm our commitment to seek the peaceful resolution of disputes as set out in the Charter of the United Nations.

* * *

Based on these foundations we will strengthen our common response and improve our common instruments in order to meet the challenges confronting us more efficiently.

III. Our Common Response

Co-operation With Other Organizations: The Platform for Co-Operative Security

12. The risks and challenges we face today cannot be met by a single State or organization. Over the last decade, we have taken important steps to forge new co-operation between the OSCE and other international organizations. In order to make full use of the resources of the international community, we are committed to even closer co-operation among international organizations.

We pledge ourselves, through the Platform for Co-operative Security, which is hereby adopted as an essential element of this Charter, to further strengthen and develop co-operation with competent organizations on the basis of equality and in a spirit of partnership. The principles of the Platform for Co-operative Security, as set out in the operational document attached to this Charter, apply to any organization or institution whose members individually and collectively decide to adhere to them. They apply across all dimensions of security; politico-military, human and economic. Through this Platform we seek to develop and maintain political and operational coherence, on the basis of shared values, among all the various bodies dealing with security, both in responding to specific crises and in formulating responses to new risks and challenges. Recognizing the key integrating role that the OSCE can play, we offer the OSCE, when appropriate, as a flexible co-ordinating framework to foster co-operation, through which various organizations can reinforce each other drawing on their particular strengths. We do not intend to create a hierarchy of organizations or a permanent division of labour among them.

We are ready in principle to deploy the resources of international organizations and institutions of which we are members in support of the OSCE's work, subject to the necessary policy decisions as cases arise.

13. Subregional co-operation has become an important element in enhancing security across the OSCE area. Processes such as the Stability Pact for South-Eastern Europe, which has been placed under the auspices of the OSCE, help to promote our common values. They contribute to improved security not just in the subregion in question but throughout the OSCE area. We offer the OSCE, in accordance with the Platform for Co-operative Security, as a forum for subregional co-operation. In this respect, and in accordance with the modalities in the operational document, the OSCE will facilitate the exchange of information and experience between subregional groups and may, if so requested, receive and keep their mutual accords and agreements.

Solidarity and Partnership

14. Peace and security in our region is best guaranteed by the willingness and ability of each participating State to uphold democracy, the rule of law and respect for human rights. We individually confirm our willingness to comply fully with our commitments. We also have a joint responsibility to uphold OSCE principles. We are therefore determined to co-operate within the OSCE and with its institutions and representatives and stand ready to use OSCE instruments, tools and mechanisms. We will co-operate in a spirit of solidarity and partnership in a continuing review of implementation. Today we commit ourselves to joint measures based on co-operation, both in the OSCE and through those organizations of which we are members, in order to offer assistance to participating States to enhance their compliance with OSCE principles and commitments. We will strengthen existing co-operative instruments and develop new ones in order to respond efficiently to requests for assistance from participating States. We will explore ways to further increase the effectiveness of the Organization to deal with cases of clear, gross and continuing violations of those principles and commitments.

15. We are determined to consider ways of helping participating States requesting assistance in cases of internal breakdown of law and order. We will jointly examine the nature of the situation and possible ways and means of providing support to the State in question.

16. We reaffirm the validity of the Code of Conduct on Politico-Military Aspects of Security. We will consult promptly, in conformity with our OSCE responsibilities, with a participating State seeking assistance in realizing its right to individual or collective self-defence in the event that its sovereignty, territorial integrity and political independence are threatened. We will consider jointly the nature of the threat and actions that may be required in defence of our common values.

Our Institutions

17. The Parliamentary Assembly has developed into one of the most important OSCE institutions continuously providing new ideas and proposals. We welcome this increasing role, particularly in the field of democratic development and election monitoring. We call on the Parliamentary Assembly to develop its activities further as a key component in our efforts to promote democracy, prosperity and increased confidence within and between participating States.

18. The Office for Democratic Institutions and Human Rights (ODIHR), the High Commissioner on National Minorities (HCNM) and the Representative on Freedom of the Media are essential instruments in ensuring respect for human rights, democracy and the rule of law. The OSCE Secretariat provides vital assistance to the Chairman-in-Office and to the activities of our Organization, especially in the field. We will also strengthen further the operational capacities of the OSCE Secretariat to enable it to face the expansion of our activities and to ensure that field operations function effectively and in accordance with the mandates and guidance given to them.

We commit ourselves to giving the OSCE institutions our full support. We emphasize the importance of close co-ordination among the OSCE institutions, as well as our field operations, in order to make optimal use of our common resources. We will take into account the need for geographic diversity and gender balance when recruiting personnel to OSCE institutions and field operations.

We acknowledge the tremendous developments and diversification of OSCE activities. We recognize that a large number of OSCE participating States have not been able to implement the 1993 decision of the Rome Ministerial Council, and that difficulties can arise from the absence of a legal capacity of the Organization. We will seek to improve the situation.

The Human Dimension

19. We reaffirm that respect for human rights and fundamental freedoms, democracy and the rule of law is at the core of the OSCE's comprehensive concept of security. We commit ourselves to counter such threats to security as violations of human rights and fundamental freedoms, including the freedom of thought, conscience, religion or belief and manifestations of intolerance, aggressive nationalism, racism, chauvinism, xenophobia and anti-semitism.

The protection and promotion of the rights of persons belonging to national minorities are essential factors for democracy, peace, justice and stability within, and between, participating States. In this respect we reaffirm our commitments, in particular under the relevant provisions of the Copenhagen 1990 Human Dimension Document, and recall the Report of the Geneva 1991 Meeting of Experts on National Minorities. Full respect for human rights, including the rights of persons belonging to national minorities, besides being an end in itself, may not undermine, but strengthen territorial integrity and sovereignty. Various concepts of autonomy as well as other approaches outlined in the above-mentioned documents, which are in line with OSCE principles, constitute ways to preserve and promote the ethnic, cultural, linguistic and religious identity of national minorities within an existing State. We condemn violence against any minority. We pledge to take measures to promote tolerance and to build pluralistic societies where all, regardless of their ethnic origin, enjoy full equality of opportunity. We emphasize that questions relating to national minorities can only be satisfactorily resolved in a democratic political framework based on the rule of law.

We reaffirm our recognition that everyone has the right to a nationality and that no one should be deprived of his or her nationality arbitrarily. We commit ourselves to continue our efforts to ensure that everyone can exercise this right. We also commit ourselves to further the international protection of stateless persons.

20. We recognize the particular difficulties faced by Roma and Sinti and the need to undertake effective measures in order to achieve full equality of opportunity, consistent with OSCE commitments, for persons belonging to Roma and Sinti. We will reinforce our efforts to ensure that Roma and Sinti are able to play a full and equal part in our societies, and to eradicate discrimination against them.

21. We are committed to eradicating torture and cruel, inhumane or degrading treatment or punishment throughout the OSCE area. To this end, we will promote legislation to provide procedural and substantive safeguards and remedies to combat these practices. We will assist victims and co-operate with relevant international organizations and non-governmental organizations, as appropriate.

22. We reject any policy of ethnic cleansing or mass expulsion. We reaffirm our commitment to respect the right to seek asylum and to ensure the international protection of refugees as set out in the 1951 Convention Relating to the Status of Refugees and its 1967 Protocol, as well as to facilitate the voluntary return of refugees and internally displaced persons in dignity and safety. We will pursue without discrimination the reintegration of refugees and internally displaced persons in their places of origin.

In order to enhance the protection of civilians in times of conflict, we will seek ways of reinforcing the application of international humanitarian law.

23. The full and equal exercise by women of their human rights is essential to achieve a more peaceful, prosperous and democratic OSCE area. We are committed to making equality between men and women an integral part of our policies, both at the level of our States and within the Organization.

24. We will undertake measures to eliminate all forms of discrimination against women, and to end violence against women and children as well as sexual

exploitation and all forms of trafficking in human beings. In order to prevent such crimes we will, among other means, promote the adoption or strengthening of legislation to hold accountable persons responsible for these acts and strengthen the protection of victims. We will also develop and implement measures to promote the rights and interests of children in armed conflict and post-conflict situations, including refugees and internally displaced children. We will look at ways of preventing forced or compulsory recruitment for use in armed conflict of persons under 18 years of age.

25. We reaffirm our obligation to conduct free and fair elections in accordance with OSCE commitments, in particular the Copenhagen Document 1990. We recognize the assistance the ODIHR can provide to participating States in developing and implementing electoral legislation. In line with these commitments, we will invite observers to our elections from other participating States, the ODIHR, the OSCE Parliamentary Assembly and appropriate institutions and organizations that wish to observe our election proceedings. We agree to follow up promptly the ODIHR's election assessment and recommendations.

26. We reaffirm the importance of independent media and the free flow of information as well as the public's access to information. We commit ourselves to take all necessary steps to ensure the basic conditions for free and independent media and unimpeded transborder and intra-State flow of information, which we consider to be an essential component of any democratic, free and open society.

27. Non-governmental organizations (NGOs) can perform a vital role in the promotion of human rights, democracy and the rule of law. They are an integral component of a strong civil society. We pledge ourselves to enhance the ability of NGOs to make their full contribution to the further development of civil society and respect for human rights and fundamental freedoms.

The Politico-Military Dimension

28. The politico-military aspects of security remain vital to the interests of participating States. They constitute a core element of the OSCE's concept of comprehensive security. Disarmament, arms control and confidence- and security-building measures (CSBMs) are important parts of the overall effort to enhance security by fostering stability, transparency and predictability in the military field. Full implementation, timely adaptation and, when required, further development of arms control agreements and CSBMs are key contributions to our political and military stability.

29. The Treaty on Conventional Armed Forces in Europe (CFE) must continue to serve as a cornerstone of European security. It has dramatically reduced equipment levels. It provides a fundamental contribution to a more secure and integrated

Europe. The States Parties to this Treaty are taking a critical step forward. The Treaty is being strengthened by adapting its provisions to ensure enhanced stability, predictability and transparency amidst changing circumstances. A number of States Parties will reduce further their equipment levels. The adapted Treaty, upon its entry into force, will be open to voluntary accession by other OSCE participating States in the area between the Atlantic Ocean and the Ural Mountains and thereby will provide an important additional contribution to European stability and security.

30. The OSCE Vienna Document 1999, together with other documents adopted by the Forum for Security Co-operation (FSC) on politico-military aspects of security, provide valuable tools for all OSCE participating States in building greater mutual confidence and military transparency. We will continue to make regular use of and fully implement all OSCE instruments in this field and seek their timely adaptation in order to ensure adequate response to security needs in the OSCE area. We remain committed to the principles contained in the Code of Conduct on politico-military aspects of security. We are determined to make further efforts within the FSC in order to jointly address common security concerns of participating States and to pursue the OSCE's concept of comprehensive and indivisible security so far as the politico-military dimension is concerned. We will continue a substantial security dialogue and task our representatives to conduct this dialogue in the framework of the FSC.

The Economic and Environmental Dimension

31. The link between security, democracy and prosperity has become increasingly evident in the OSCE area, as has the risk to security from environmental degradation and the depletion of natural resources. Economic liberty, social justice and environmental responsibility are indispensable for prosperity. On the basis of these linkages, we will ensure that the economic dimension receives appropriate attention, in particular as an element of our early warning and conflict prevention activities. We will do so, inter alia, with a view to promoting the integration of economies in transition into the world economy and to ensure the rule of law and the development of a transparent and stable legal system in the economic sphere.

32. The OSCE is characterized by its broad membership, its comprehensive approach to security, its large number of field operations and its long history as a norm-setting organization. These qualities enable it to identify threats and to act as a catalyst for co-operation between key international organizations and institutions in the economic and environmental areas. The OSCE stands ready to play this role, where appropriate. We will foster such co-ordination between the OSCE and relevant international organizations in accordance with the Platform for Co-operative Security. We will enhance the OSCE's ability to address economic and environmental issues in ways that neither duplicate existing work nor replace

efforts that can be more efficiently undertaken by other organizations. We will focus on areas in which the OSCE has particular competence. The OSCE's efforts within the human dimension have significant economic effects and vice versa, for example by mobilizing human resources and talents and by helping to build vibrant civil societies. In the spirit of the 1998 Århus Convention on Access to Information, Public Participation in Decision-Making and Access to Justice in Environmental Matters, we will in particular seek to ensure access to information, public participation in decision-making and access to justice in environmental matters.

Rule of Law and Fight Against Corruption

33. We reaffirm our commitment to the rule of law. We recognize that corruption poses a great threat to the OSCE's shared values. It generates instability and reaches into many aspects of the security, economic and human dimensions. Participating States pledge to strengthen their efforts to combat corruption and the conditions that foster it, and to promote a positive framework for good government practices and public integrity. They will make better use of existing international instruments and assist each other in their fight against corruption. As part of its work to promote the rule of law, the OSCE will work with NGOs that are committed to a strong public and business consensus against corrupt practices.

IV. Our Common Instruments

Enhancing Our Dialogue

34. We are determined to broaden and strengthen our dialogue concerning developments related to all aspects of security in the OSCE area. We charge the Permanent Council and the FSC within their respective areas of competence to address in greater depth security concerns of the participating States and to pursue the OSCE's concept of comprehensive and indivisible security.

35. The Permanent Council, being the regular body for political consultations and decision-making, will address the full range of conceptual issues as well as the day-to-day operational work of the Organization. To assist in its deliberations and decision-making and to strengthen the process of political consultations and transparency within the Organization, we will establish a Preparatory Committee under the Permanent Council's direction. This open-ended Committee will normally meet in informal format and will be tasked by the Council, or its Chairman, to deliberate and to report back to the Council.

36. Reflecting our spirit of solidarity and partnership, we will also enhance our political dialogue in order to offer assistance to participating States, thereby

ensuring compliance with OSCE commitments. To encourage this dialogue, we have decided, in accordance with established rules and practices, to make increased use of OSCE instruments, including:

- Dispatching delegations from the OSCE institutions, with the participation of other relevant international organizations, when appropriate, to provide advice and expertise for reform of legislation and practices;
- Dispatching Personal Representatives of the Chairman-in-Office, after consultations with the State concerned, for fact-finding or advisory missions;
- Bringing together representatives of the OSCE and States concerned in order to address questions regarding compliance with OSCE commitments;
- Organizing training programmes aimed at improving standards and practices, inter alia, within the fields of human rights, democratization and the rule of law;
- Addressing matters regarding compliance with OSCE commitments at OSCE review meetings and conferences as well as in the Economic Forum;
- Submitting such matters for consideration by the Permanent Council, inter alia, on the basis of recommendations by the OSCE institutions within their respective mandates or by Personal Representatives of the Chairman-in-Office;
- Convening meetings of the Permanent Council in a special or reinforced format in order to discuss matters of non-compliance with OSCE commitments and to decide on appropriate courses of action;
- Establishing field operations with the consent of the State concerned.

OSCE Field Operations

37. The Permanent Council will establish field operations. It will decide on their mandates and budgets. On this basis, the Permanent Council and the Chairman-in-Office will provide guidance to such operations.

38. The development of OSCE field operations represents a major transformation of the Organization that has enabled the OSCE to play a more prominent role in promoting peace, security and compliance with OSCE commitments. Based on the experience we have acquired, we will develop and strengthen this instrument further in order to carry out tasks according to their respective mandates, which may, inter alia, include the following:

- Providing assistance and advice or formulating recommendations in areas agreed by the OSCE and the host country;
- Observing compliance with OSCE commitments and providing advice or recommendations for improved compliance;
- Assisting in the organization and monitoring of elections;
- Providing support for the primacy of law and democratic institutions and for the maintenance and restoration of law and order;

- Helping to create conditions for negotiation or other measures that could facilitate the peaceful settlement of conflicts;
- Verifying and/or assisting in fulfilling agreements on the peaceful settlement of conflicts;
- Providing support in the rehabilitation and reconstruction of various aspects of society.

39. Recruitment to field operations must ensure that qualified personnel are made available by participating States. The training of personnel is an important aspect of enhancing the effectiveness of the OSCE and its field operations and will therefore be improved. Existing training facilities in OSCE participating States and training activities of the OSCE could play an active role in achieving this aim in co-operation, where appropriate, with other organizations and institutions.

40. In accordance with the Platform for Co-operative Security, co-operation between OSCE and other international organizations in performing field operations will be enhanced. This will be done, inter alia, by carrying out common projects with other partners, in particular the Council of Europe, allowing the OSCE to benefit from their expertise while respecting the identity and decision-making procedures of each organization involved.

41. The host country of an OSCE field operation should, when appropriate, be assisted in building its own capacity and expertise within the area of responsibility. This would facilitate an efficient transfer of the tasks of the operation to the host country, and consequently the closure of the field operation.

Rapid Response (REACT)

42. We recognize that the ability to deploy rapidly civilian and police expertise is essential to effective conflict prevention, crisis management and post-conflict rehabilitation. We are committed to developing a capability within the participating States and the OSCE to set up Rapid Expert Assistance and Co-operation Teams (REACT) that will be at the disposal of the OSCE. This will enable OSCE bodies and institutions, acting in accordance with their respective procedures, to offer experts quickly to OSCE participating States to provide assistance, in compliance with OSCE norms, in conflict prevention, crisis management and post-conflict rehabilitation. This rapidly deployable capability will cover a wide range of civilian expertise. It will give us the ability to address problems before they become crises and to deploy quickly the civilian component of a peacekeeping operation when needed. These Teams could also be used as surge capacity to assist the OSCE with the rapid deployment of large-scale or specialized operations. We expect REACT to develop and evolve, along with other OSCE capabilities, to meet the needs of the Organization.

Operation Centre

43. Rapid deployment is important for the OSCE's effectiveness in contributing to our conflict prevention, crisis management and post-conflict rehabilitation efforts and depends on effective preparation and planning. To facilitate this, we decide to set up an Operation Centre within the Conflict Prevention Centre with a small core staff, having expertise relevant for all kinds of OSCE operations, which can be expanded rapidly when required. Its role will be to plan and deploy field operations, including those involving REACT resources. It will liaise with other international organizations and institutions as appropriate in accordance with the Platform for Co-operative Security. The Centre's core staff will, to the extent possible, be drawn from personnel with appropriate expertise seconded by participating States and from existing Secretariat resources. This core will provide the basis for rapid expansion, to deal with new tasks as they arise. The precise arrangements will be decided in accordance with existing procedures.

Police-Related Activities

44. We will work to enhance the OSCE's role in civilian police-related activities as an integral part of the Organization's efforts in conflict prevention, crisis management and post-conflict rehabilitation. Such activities may comprise:

- Police monitoring, including with the aim of preventing police from carrying out such activities as discrimination based on religious and ethnic identity;
- Police training, which could, inter alia, include the following tasks:
- Improving the operational and tactical capabilities of local police services and reforming paramilitary forces;
- Providing new and modern policing skills, such as community policing, and anti-drug, anti-corruption and anti-terrorist capacities;
- Creating a police service with a multi-ethnic and/or multi-religious composition that can enjoy the confidence of the entire population;
- Promoting respect for human rights and fundamental freedoms in general.

We will encourage the provision of modern equipment appropriate to police services that receive training in such new skills.

In addition, the OSCE will examine options and conditions for a role in law enforcement.

45. We shall also promote the development of independent judicial systems that play a key role in providing remedies for human rights violations as well as providing advice and assistance for prison system reforms. The OSCE will also work with other international organizations in the creation of political and legal frameworks within which the police can perform its tasks in accordance with democratic principles and the rule of law.

Peacekeeping

46. We remain committed to reinforcing the OSCE's key role in maintaining peace and stability throughout our area. The OSCE's most effective contributions to regional security have been in areas such as field operations, post-conflict rehabilitation, democratization, and human rights and election monitoring. We have decided to explore options for a potentially greater and wider role for the OSCE in peacekeeping. Reaffirming our rights and obligations under the Charter of the United Nations, and on the basis of our existing decisions, we confirm that the OSCE can, on a case-by-case basis and by consensus, decide to play a role in peacekeeping, including a leading role when participating States judge it to be the most effective and appropriate organization. In this regard, it could also decide to provide the mandate covering peacekeeping by others and seek the support of participating States as well as other organizations to provide resources and expertise. In accordance with the Platform for Co-operative Security, it could also provide a co-ordinating framework for such efforts.

The Court of Conciliation and Arbitration

47. We reiterate that the principle of the peaceful settlement of disputes is at the core of OSCE commitments. The Court of Conciliation and Arbitration, in this respect, remains a tool available to those, a large number of participating States, which have become parties to the 1992 Convention of Stockholm. We encourage them to use this instrument to resolve disputes between them, as well as with other participating States which voluntarily submit to the jurisdiction of the Court. We also encourage those participating States which have not yet done so to consider joining the Convention.

V. OUR PARTNERS FOR CO-OPERATION

48. We recognize the interdependence between the security of the OSCE area and that of Partners for Co-operation, as well as our commitment to the relationship and the dialogue with them. We emphasize in particular the long-standing relations with our Mediterranean partners, Algeria, Egypt, Israel, Jordan, Morocco and Tunisia. We recognize the increased involvement in and support for the work of the OSCE by our Partners for Co-operation. Building on this interdependence, we are ready to develop this process further. Implementing and building on the Helsinki Document 1992 and the Budapest Document 1994, we will work more closely with the Partners for Co-operation to promote OSCE norms and principles. We welcome their wish to promote the realization of the Organization's norms and principles, including the fundamental principle of resolving conflicts through peaceful means. To this end, we will invite the Partners for Co-operation on a

more regular basis to increased participation in the work of the OSCE as the dialogue develops.

49. The potential of the Contact Group and the Mediterranean seminars must be fully explored and exploited. Drawing on the Budapest mandate, the Permanent Council will examine the recommendations emerging from the Contact Group and the Mediterranean seminars. We will encourage the Mediterranean Partners for Co-operation to draw on our expertise in setting up structures and mechanisms in the Mediterranean for early warning, preventive diplomacy and conflict prevention.

50. We welcome the increased participation in our work by Japan and the Republic of Korea. We welcome the contribution by Japan to OSCE field activities. We will seek to strengthen further our co-operation with our Asian partners in meeting challenges of common interest.

VI. Conclusion

51. This Charter will benefit the security of all participating States by enhancing and strengthening the OSCE as we enter the twenty-first century. Today we have decided to develop its existing instruments and to create new tools. We will use them fully to promote a free, democratic and secure OSCE area. The Charter will thus underpin the OSCE's role as the only pan-European security organization entrusted with ensuring peace and stability in its area. We appreciate the completion of the work of the Security Model Committee.

52. The original of the present Charter, drawn up in English, French, German, Italian, Russian and Spanish, will be transmitted to the Secretary General of the Organization, who will transmit a certified true copy of this Charter to each of the participating States.

We, the undersigned High Representatives of the participating States, mindful of the high political significance that we attach to the present Charter and declaring our determination to act in accordance with the provisions contained in the above text, have subscribed our signatures below.

OPERATIONAL DOCUMENT –
THE PLATFORM FOR CO-OPERATIVE SECURITY

I. The Platform

1. The goal of the Platform for Co-operative Security is to strengthen the mutually reinforcing nature of the relationship between those organizations and institutions concerned with the promotion of comprehensive security within the OSCE area.

2. The OSCE will work co-operatively with those organizations and institutions whose members individually and collectively, in a manner consistent with the modalities appropriate to each organization or institution, now and in the future:

- Adhere to the principles of the Charter of the United Nations and the OSCE principles and commitments as set out in the Helsinki Final Act, the Charter of Paris, the Helsinki Document 1992, the Budapest Document 1994, the OSCE Code of Conduct on politico-military aspects of security and the Lisbon Declaration on a Common and Comprehensive Security Model for Europe for the twenty-first century;
- Subscribe to the principles of transparency and predictability in their actions in the spirit of the Vienna Document 1999 of the Negotiations on Confidence- and Security-Building Measures;
- Implement fully the arms control obligations, including disarmament and CSBMs, to which they have committed themselves;
- Proceed on the basis that those organizations and institutions of which they are members will adhere to transparency about their evolution;
- Ensure that their membership in those organizations and institutions is based on openness and free will;
- Actively support the OSCE's concept of common, comprehensive and indivisible security and a common security space free of dividing lines;
- Play a full and appropriate part in the development of the relationships between mutually reinforcing security-related institutions in the OSCE area;
- Are ready in principle to deploy the institutional resources of international organizations and institutions of which they are members in support of the OSCE's work, subject to the necessary policy decisions as cases arise. In this regard, participating States note the particular relevance of co-operation in the areas of conflict prevention and crisis management.

3. Together these principles and commitments form the Platform for Co-operative Security.

II. Modalities for Co-operation

4. Within the relevant organizations and institutions of which they are members, participating States will work to ensure the organizations' and institutions' adherence to the Platform for Co-operative Security. Adherence, on the basis of decisions taken by each member State within relevant organizations and institutions, will take place in a manner consistent with the modalities appropriate to each organization or institution. Contacts and co-operation of the OSCE with other organizations and institutions will be transparent to participating States and will take place in a manner consistent with the modalities appropriate to the OSCE and those organizations and institutions.

5. At the 1997 Ministerial Meeting in Copenhagen, a decision was taken on the Common Concept for the Development of Co-operation between Mutually Reinforcing Institutions. We acknowledge the extensive network of contacts elaborated since then, in particular the growing co-operation with organizations and institutions active both in the politico-military field and in the human and economic dimensions of security, and the strengthening of co-operation between the OSCE and the various United Nations bodies and agencies, recalling the OSCE's role as a regional arrangement under the Charter of the United Nations. We are determined to develop this further.

6. The growing importance of subregional groupings in the work of the OSCE is another important area, and we support the growth in co-operation with these groups based on this Platform.

7. Development of co-operation can be further enhanced through extensive use of the following instruments and mechanisms:

- Regular contacts, including meetings; a continuous framework for dialogue; increased transparency and practical co-operation, including the identification of liaison officers or points of contact; cross-representation at appropriate meetings; and other contacts intended to increase understanding of each organization's conflict prevention tools.

8. In addition, the OSCE may engage in special meetings with other organizations, institutions and structures operating in the OSCE area. These meetings may be held at a political and/or executive level (to co-ordinate policies or determine areas of co-operation) and at a working level (to address the modalities of co-operation).

9. The development of the OSCE field operations in recent years has represented a major transformation of the Organization. In view of the adoption of the Platform for Co-operative Security, existing co-operation between the OSCE and other relevant international bodies, organizations and institutions in field operations

should be developed and built upon in accordance with their individual mandates. Modalities for this form of co-operation could include: regular information exchanges and meetings, joint needs assessment missions, secondment of experts by other organizations to the OSCE, appointment of liaison officers, development of common projects and field operations, and joint training efforts.

10. Co-operation in responding to specific crises:

- The OSCE, through its Chairman-in-Office and supported by the Secretary General, and the relevant organizations and institutions are encouraged to keep each other informed of what actions they are undertaking or plan to undertake to deal with a particular situation;
- To this end, participating States encourage the Chairman-in-Office, supported by the Secretary General, to work with other organizations and institutions to foster co-ordinated approaches that avoid duplication and ensure efficient use of available resources. As appropriate, the OSCE can offer to serve as a flexible framework for co-operation of the various mutually reinforcing efforts. The Chairman-in-Office will consult with participating States on the process and will act in accordance with the results of these consultations.

11. The Secretary General shall prepare an annual report for the Permanent Council on interaction between organizations and institutions in the OSCE area.

Stability Pact for South-Eastern Europe, Cologne, 10 June 1999

I. Participants, Description of Situation

1. We, the Foreign Ministers of the Member States of the European Union, the European Commission, the Foreign Ministers of Albania, Bosnia and Herzegovina, Bulgaria, Croatia, Hungary, Romania, the Russian Federation, Slovenia, the former Yugoslav Republic of Macedonia, Turkey, the United States of America, the OSCE Chairman in Office and the Representative of the Council of Europe representing the participants in today's Conference on South Eastern Europe; and the Foreign Ministers of Canada and Japan, Representatives of the United Nations, UNHCR, NATO, OECD, WEU, International Monetary Fund, the World Bank, the European Investment Bank and the European Bank for Reconstruction and Development, acting within their competences, representing the facilitating States, Organisations and Institutions of today's Conference, as well as the Representatives of the Royaumont process, BSEC, CEI, SECI and SEECP, have met in Cologne on 10 June 1999, in response to the European Union's call to adopt a Stability Pact for South Eastern Europe.

2. The countries of South Eastern Europe recognize their responsibility to work within the international community to develop a shared strategy for stability and growth of the region and to cooperate with each other and major donors to implement that strategy. Seizing the opportunity to address structural shortfalls and unresolved issues will accelerate democratic and economic development in the region.

3. We will strive to achieve the objective of lasting peace, prosperity and stability for South Eastern Europe. We will reach this objective through a comprehensive and coherent approach to the region involving the EU, the OSCE, the Council of Europe, the UN, NATO, the OECD, the WEU, the IFIs and the regional initiatives. We welcome the fact that the European Union and the United States have made support for the Stability Pact a priority in their New Transatlantic Agenda, as well as the fact that the European Union and the Russian Federation have made the Stability Pact a priority in their political dialogue.

4. A settlement of the Kosovo conflict is critical to our ability to reach fully the objectives of the Stability Pact and to work towards permanent, long term

measures for a future of peace and inter-ethnic harmony without fear of the resurgence of war.

II. Principles and Norms

5. We solemnly reaffirm our commitment to all the principles and norms enshrined in the UN Charter, the Helsinki Final Act, the Charter of Paris, the 1990 Copenhagen Document and other OSCE documents, and, as applicable, to full implementation of relevant UN Security Council Resolutions, the relevant conventions of the Council of Europe and the General Framework Agreement for Peace in Bosnia and Herzegovina, with a view to promoting good neighbourly relations.

6. In our endeavours, we will build upon bilateral and multilateral agreements on good neighbourly relations concluded by States in the region participating in the Pact, and will seek the conclusion of such agreements where they do not exist. They will form an essential element of the Stability Pact.

7. We reaffirm that we are accountable to our citizens and responsible to one another for respect for OSCE norms and principles and for the implementation of our commitments. We also reaffirm that commitments with respect to the human dimension undertaken through our membership in the OSCE are matters of direct and legitimate concern to all States participating in the Stability Pact, and do not belong exclusively to the internal affairs of the State concerned. Respect for these commitments constitutes one of the foundations of international order, to which we intend to make a substantial contribution.

8. We take note that countries in the region participating in the Stability Pact commit themselves to continued democratic and economic reforms, as elaborated in paragraph 10, as well as bilateral and regional cooperation amongst themselves to advance their integration, on an individual basis, into Euro-Atlantic structures. The EU Member States and other participating countries and international organisations and institutions commit themselves to making every effort to assist them to make speedy and measurable progress along this road. We reaffirm the inherent right of each and every participating State to be free to choose or change its security arrangements, including treaties of alliance as they evolve. Each participating State will respect the rights of all others in this regard. They will not strengthen their security at the expense of the security of other States.

III. Objectives

9. The Stability Pact aims at strengthening countries in South Eastern Europe in their efforts to foster peace, democracy, respect for human rights and economic prosperity, in order to achieve stability in the whole region. Those countries in the region who seek integration into Euro-Atlantic structures, alongside a number of other participants in the Pact, strongly believe that the implementation of this process will facilitate their objective.

10. To that end we pledge to cooperate towards:

- preventing and putting an end to tensions and crises as a prerequisite for lasting stability. This includes concluding and implementing among ourselves multilateral and bilateral agreements and taking domestic measures to overcome the existing potential for conflict;
- bringing about mature democratic political processes, based on free and fair elections, grounded in the rule of law and full respect for human rights and fundamental freedoms, including the rights of persons belonging to national minorities, the right to free and independent media, legislative branches accountable to their constituents, independent judiciaries, combating corruption, deepening and strengthening of civil society;
- creating peaceful and good-neighbourly relations in the region through strict observance of the principles of the Helsinki Final Act, confidence building and reconciliation, encouraging work in the OSCE and other fora on regional confidence building measures and mechanisms for security cooperation;
- preserving the multinational and multiethnic diversity of countries in the region, and protecting minorities;
- creating vibrant market economies based on sound macro policies, markets open to greatly expanded foreign trade and private sector investment, effective and transparent customs and commercial/regulatory regimes, developing strong capital markets and diversified ownership, including privatisation, leading to a widening circle of prosperity for all our citizens;
- fostering economic cooperation in the region and between the region and the rest of Europe and the world, including free trade areas; promoting unimpeded contacts among citizens;
- combating organised crime, corruption and terrorism and all criminal and illegal activities;
- preventing forced population displacement caused by war, persecution and civil strife as well as migration generated by poverty;
- ensuring the safe and free return of all refugees and displaced persons to their homes, while assisting the countries in the region by sharing the burden imposed upon them;
- creating the conditions, for countries of South Eastern Europe, for full integration into political, economic and security structures of their choice.

11. Lasting peace and stability in South Eastern Europe will only become possible when democratic principles and values, which are already actively promoted by many countries in the region, have taken root throughout, including in the Federal Republic of Yugoslavia. International efforts must focus on consolidating and linking areas of stability in the region to lay a firm foundation for the transition of the region as a whole to a peaceful and democratic future. We declare that the Federal Republic of Yugoslavia will be welcome as a full and equal participant in the Stability Pact, following the political settlement of the Kosovo crisis on the basis of the principles agreed by G8 Foreign Ministers and taking into account the need for respect by all participants for the principles and objectives of this Pact. In order to draw the Federal Republic of Yugoslavia closer to this goal, respecting its sovereignty and territorial integrity, we will consider ways of making the Republic of Montenegro an early beneficiary of the Pact. In this context, we welcome involvement in our meetings of representatives of Montenegro, as a constituent Republic of the Federal Republic of Yugoslavia. We also note the intention of the European Union and other interested participants to continue to work closely with its democratically elected government.

IV. Mechanisms of the Stability Pact

12. To reach the objectives we have set for ourselves, we have agreed to set up a South Eastern Europe Regional Table. The South Eastern Europe Regional Table will review progress under the Stability Pact, carry it forward and provide guidance for advancing its objectives.

13. The Stability Pact will have a Special Coordinator, who will be appointed by the European Union, after consultation with the OSCE Chairman in Office and other participants, and endorsed by the OSCE Chairman in Office. The Special Coordinator will chair the South Eastern Europe Regional Table and will be responsible for promoting achievement of the Pact's objectives within and between the individual countries, supported by appropriate structures tailored to need, in close cooperation with the governments and relevant institutions of the countries, in particular other interested associated countries of the European Union, as well as relevant international organisations and institutions concerned. The Special Coordinator will provide periodic progress reports to the OSCE, according to its procedures, on behalf of the South Eastern Europe Regional Table.

14. The South Eastern Europe Regional Table will ensure coordination of activities of and among the following Working Tables, which will build upon existing expertise, institutions and initiatives and could be divided into sub-tables:

- Working Table on democratisation and human rights;
- Working Table on economic reconstruction, development and cooperation;
- Working Table on security issues.

15. Responsibilities for these Working Tables are referred to in the Annex to this document. The Working Tables will address and facilitate the resolution of the issues entrusted to them by arrangements to be agreed at each table.

16. The South Eastern Europe Regional Table and the Working Tables will consist of the participants of the Stability Pact. The facilitator States, Organisations and Institutions as well as the regional initiatives referred to in paragraph 1 of this document are entitled to participate in the Working Tables and in the South Eastern Europe Regional Table if they so wish. Neighbouring and other countries, in particular other interested associated countries of the EU, as well as relevant international organisations and institutions may be invited as participants or observers, as appropriate, and without any ensuing commitment to the future, to the South Eastern Europe Regional Table and/or the Working Tables, in order to contribute to the objectives of the Stability Pact.

V. Roles of and Cooperation Between Participants

17. Work in the Stability Pact should take into account the diversity of the situation of participants. To achieve the objectives of this Pact, we will provide for effective coordination between the participating and facilitating States, international and regional Organisations and Institutions, which have unique knowledge and expertise to contribute to the common endeavour. We look to the active and creative participation by all concerned to bring about the conditions which will enable the countries in the region to seize the opportunity represented by this Pact. Each of the participants will endeavour to ensure that the objectives of the Stability Pact are furthered in their own participation in all relevant international Organisations and Institutions.

Role of the EU

18. We welcome the European Union's initiative in launching the Stability Pact and the leading role the EU is playing, in cooperation with other participating and facilitating States, international Organisations and Institutions. The launching of the Pact will give a firm European anchorage to the region. The ultimate success of the Pact will depend largely on the efforts of the States concerned to fulfil the objectives of the Pact and to develop regional cooperation through multilateral and bilateral agreements.

19. We warmly welcome the European Union's readiness to actively support the countries in the region and to enable them to achieve the objectives of the Stability Pact. We welcome the EU's activity to strengthen democratic and economic institutions in the region through a number of relevant programmes. We note progress towards the establishment and development of contractual relations, on an individual basis and within the framework of its Regional Approach, between the EU and countries of the region. We take note that, on the basis of the Vienna European Council Conclusions, the EU will prepare a 'Common Strategy towards the Western Balkans', as a fundamental initiative.

20. The EU will draw the region closer to the perspective of full integration of these countries into its structures. In case of countries which have not yet concluded association agreements with the EU, this will be done through a new kind of contractual relationship taking fully into account the individual situations of each country with the perspective of EU membership, on the basis of the Amsterdam Treaty and once the Copenhagen criteria have been met. We note the European Union's willingness that, while deciding autonomously, it will consider the achievement of the objectives of the Stability Pact, in particular progress in developing regional cooperation, among the important elements in evaluating the merits of such a perspective.

Role of Countries in the Region

21. We highly appreciate the contribution and the solidarity of the countries in the region with the efforts of the international community for reaching a peaceful solution on Kosovo. We welcome the efforts so far deployed and results achieved by countries in South Eastern Europe towards democratisation, economic reform and regional cooperation and stability. These countries will be the main beneficiaries of the Pact and recognise that its successful implementation, and the advance towards Euro-Atlantic structures for those seeking it depend decisively on their commitment to implement the objectives of the Pact, in particular on their willingness to cooperate on a bilateral and multilateral level and to promote the objectives of the Pact within their own respective national structures.

Role of the OSCE

22. We welcome the OSCE's intention, as the only pan-European security organisation and as a regional arrangement under Chapter VIII of the UN Charter and a primary instrument for early warning, conflict prevention, crisis management and post-conflict rehabilitation, to make a significant contribution to the efforts undertaken through the Stability Pact. We reaffirm that the OSCE has a key role to play in fostering all dimensions of security and stability. Accordingly, we request that the Stability Pact be placed under the auspices of the OSCE, and will rely fully on the OSCE to work for compliance with the provisions of the Stability Pact by

the participating States, in accordance with its procedures and established principles.

23. We will rely on the OSCE institutions and instruments and their expertise to contribute to the proceedings of the South Eastern Europe Regional Table and of the Working Tables, in particular the Working Table on Democratisation and Human Rights. Their unique competences will be much needed in furthering the aims and objectives of the Stability Pact. We express our intention, in cases requiring OSCE involvement with regard to the observance of OSCE principles in the implementation of the Stability Pact, to resort, where appropriate, to the instruments and procedures of the OSCE, including those concerning conflict prevention, the peaceful settlement of disputes and the human dimension. States parties to the Convention establishing the Court of Conciliation and Arbitration may also refer to the Court possible disputes and ask for the non-binding opinion of the Court.

Role of the Council of Europe

24. We welcome the Council of Europe's readiness to integrate all countries in the region into full membership on the basis of the principles of pluralist democracy, human rights and the rule of law. The Council of Europe can make an important contribution to the objectives of the Pact through its parliamentary and intergovernmental organs and institutions, its European norms embodied in relevant legally-binding Conventions, primarily the European Convention of Human Rights (and the Court), its instruments and assistance programmes in the fields of democratic institutions, human rights, law, justice and education, as well as its strong links with civil society. In this context, we take note with great interest of the Council of Europe's Stability Programme for South East Europe to be implemented, together and in close coordination with the countries concerned and other international and regional organisations active in the field.

Role of the UN, including UNHCR

25. We underline the UN's central role in the region for peace and security and for lasting political normalisation, as well as for humanitarian efforts and economic rehabilitation. We strongly support UNHCR's lead agency function in all refugee-related questions, in particular the protection and return of refugees and displaced persons and the crucial role undertaken by WFP, UNICEF, WHO, UNDP, UNHCHR and other members of the UN system. We look forward to the active involvement of relevant UN agencies in the South Eastern Europe Regional Table. We note that the UN Economic Commission for Europe has expertise which can usefully contribute to the proceedings of the Working Tables of the Stability Pact.

Role of NATO

26. We note NATO's decision to increase cooperation with the countries of South Eastern Europe and its commitment to openness, as well as the intention of NATO, the Euro-Atlantic Partnership Council and the Partnership for Peace to work in cooperation with other Euro-Atlantic structures, to contribute to stability and security and to maintain and increase consultations with the countries of the region. We call for their engagement, in conformity with the objectives of the Pact, in regional security cooperation and conflict prevention and management. We welcome these stabilization activities aimed at promoting the objectives of this Pact. The enhanced use of NATO's consultative fora and mechanisms, the development of an EAPC cooperative mechanism and the increased use of Partnership for Peace programmes will serve the objectives of overall stability, cooperation and good-neighbourliness envisaged in the Pact.

27. The members of NATO and a substantial number of other participants underscore that the Alliance has an important role to play in achieving the objectives of the Pact, noting in particular NATO's recent decisions to reach out to countries of the region.

Role of the United States of America

28. Having worked closely with the European Union to launch this Pact, the United States of America will continue to play a leading role in the development and implementation of the Pact, in cooperation with other participants and facilitators. We believe that the active role of the United States underscores the vital importance attached by countries of the region to their integration into Euro-Atlantic structures.

We note the United States' readiness to support this objective, as these countries work to become as strong candidates as possible for eventual membership in Euro-Atlantic institutions. We welcome the ongoing contribution of the United States, including through economic and technical assistance programmes, and through its shared leadership in International financial Institutions, to the States of South Eastern Europe. The United States will coordinate and cooperate with the other donors to ensure the maximum effectiveness of assistance to the region.

Role of the Russian Federation

29. Russia has played and continues to play a key role in the region. Russian efforts and contribution to achieving a peaceful solution of conflicts there, in particular of the Kosovo crisis, are appreciated. Having been involved at an early stage in the launching of this Pact, the Russian Federation will continue to play a leading and constructive role in development and implementation of the Pact, in cooperation with the EU, the UN, the OSCE, the Council of Europe, international

economic and financial organisations and institutions, as well as regional initiatives and individual states. The Russian Federation can make a valuable contribution to activities aimed at promoting peace, security and post-conflict cooperation.

Role of the IFIs

30. The IMF, the World Bank, the EBRD and the EIB, as the European Union financing institution, have a most important role to play, in accordance with their specific mandates, in supporting the countries in the region in achieving economic stabilisation, reform, and development of the region. We rely on them to develop a coherent international assistance strategy for the region and to promote sound macro-economic and structural policies by the countries concerned. We call on these International Financial Institutions to take an active part in the South Eastern Europe Regional Table and the relevant Working Tables.

Role of the OECD

31. We note the OECD's unique strength as a forum for dialogue on medium-term structural policy and best practices. We rely on the OECD in consideration of its well-known competence in dealing with economies in transition and its open dialogue with the countries of South Eastern Europe, to take an active part in the South Eastern Europe Regional Table and to assist in the process of economic reconstruction, the strengthening of good governance and administrative capacities and the further integration of affected States into the European and global economy.

Role of the WEU

32. We welcome the role which the WEU plays in promoting stability in the region. We note in this respect the contribution to security the WEU makes, at the request of the European Union, through its missions in countries in the region.

VI. Regional Initiatives and Organisations

33. We stress our interest in viable regional initiatives and organisations which foster friendly cooperation between neighbouring States. We welcome sub-regional cooperation schemes between participating countries. We will endeavour to ensure cooperation and coordination between these initiatives and the Stability Pact, which will be mutually reinforcing. We will build on their relevant achievements.

34. We note that the Royaumont process has already established a dynamic framework for cooperation in the area of democracy and civil society. Therefore,

Royaumont has a key role to play in this area, particularly within the framework of the first Working Table of the Stability Pact.

35. We note the role of the Organization of the Black Sea Economic Cooperation in promoting mutual understanding, improving the overall political climate and fostering economic development in the Black Sea region. Welcoming its engagement to peace, security and stability through economic cooperation, we invite the BSEC to contribute to the implementation of the Stability Pact for South Eastern Europe.

36. We note that the Central European Initiative has established, with countries in the region, a stable and integrated framework of dialogue, coordination and cooperation in the political, economic, cultural and parliamentary fields. On the basis of its experience, it has an important role to play in the framework of the South Eastern Europe Regional Table.

37. We note that the South East Europe Cooperation Initiative (SECI) has developed an innovative approach to economic and infrastructure related cooperation in the region by facilitating joint decision-making by the South Eastern European countries in its areas of activity. As such, it has a key role to play concerning regional economic issues, in particular the removal of disincentives to private investment in the region, in the framework of the Stability Pact.

38. We commend the South Eastern Europe Cooperation Process as a further successful regional cooperation scheme. We encourage its further development and institutionalisation, including the finalisation of its charter on good-neighbourly relations and cooperation.

39. We note the contribution in the security dimension of the South Eastern European Defence Ministers (SEDM) group, which has brought the countries of the region and other nations into a variety of cooperative activities which enhance transparency and mutual confidence, such as the new Multinational Peace-Keeping Force for South East Europe.

40. We expect the proposed Conference on the Adriatic and Ionian Sea region to provide a positive contribution to the region.

VII. International Donor Mobilisation and Coordination Process

41. We reaffirm our strong commitment to support reconstruction, stabilisation and integration for the region, and call upon the international donor community to participate generously. We welcome the progress made by the World Bank and the European Union, through the European Commission, towards establishing a donor

coordination process. This process will closely interact with the relevant Working Table, and will identify appropriate modalities to administer and channel international assistance. The World Bank and the European Commission will also be responsible for coordinating a comprehensive approach for regional development and the necessary donors conferences.

VIII. Implementation and Review Mechanisms

42. Effective implementation of this Pact will depend on the development and the strengthening of administrative and institutional capacity as well as civil society in the countries concerned – both at national and local level – in order to reinforce the consolidation of democratic structures and have longer-term benefits for effective administration and absorption of international assistance for the region.

43. The South Eastern Europe Regional Table and the Working Tables will be convened for their inaugural meetings at the earliest possible opportunity at the invitation of the Presidency of the European Union. They will work to achieve concrete results according to agreed timelines, in conformity with the objectives of the Stability Pact. The South Eastern Europe Regional Table will meet periodically, at a level to be determined, to review progress made by the Working Tables. The South Eastern Europe Regional Table will provide guidance to the Working Tables.

Annex

Organisation of the South Eastern Europe Regional Table and the Working Tables of the Stability Pact for South Eastern Europe

A. The South Eastern Europe Regional Table will carry forward the Stability Pact by acting as a clearing house for all questions of principle relating to the substance and implementation of the Stability Pact as well as a steering body in the Stability Pact process. The South Eastern Europe Regional Table will provide guidance to the Working Tables.

B. The Working Tables are instruments for maintaining and improving good-neighbourly relations in the region by constructively addressing and facilitating the resolution of the issues entrusted to them. The objectives of the Working Tables will be in particular:

– the discussion of issues in a multilateral framework conducive to the definition of ways to address shortfalls and to the settlement of differences by arrangements and agreements, drawing on the expertise and support of

participants as well as facilitator States, Organisations, Institutions and regional initiatives, in particular from the OSCE and the Council of Europe;
- the identification of projects aimed at facilitating the achievement of arrangements, agreements and measures in conformity with the objectives of the Pact. Special attention is to be given to projects which involve two and more countries in the region.
- where necessary, the injection of momentum in areas where further progress should be achieved.

C. Each Working Table will address the following range of issues and will decide, as appropriate, whether the establishment of sub-tables, comprising the participants and facilitators, will be necessary;

- Working Table on democratisation and human rights, which will address:

    (i) democratisation and human rights, including the rights of persons belonging to national minorities; free and independent media; civil society building; rule of law and law enforcement; institution building; efficient administration and good governance; development of common rules of conduct on border related questions; other related questions of interest to the participants;
    (ii) refugee issues, including protection and return of refugees and displaced persons;

- Working Table on economic reconstruction, development and cooperation, including economic cooperation in the region and between the region and the rest of Europe and the world; promotion of free trade areas; border-crossing transport; energy supply and savings; deregulation and transparency; infrastructure; promotion of private sector business; environmental issues; sustainable reintegration of refugees; other related questions of interest to the participants, while maintaining the integrity of the donor coordination process;

- Working Table on security issues, which will:

    (i) address justice and home affairs, as well as migratory issues; focus on measures to combat organized crime, corruption, terrorism and all criminal and illegal activities, transboundary environmental hazards; other related questions of interest to the participants;
    (ii) receive regular information from the competent bodies addressing transparency and confidence- building measures in the region. This Table will also encourage continued implementation of the Dayton/Paris Article IV Arms Control Agreement and progress of the negotiations of Article V, and should consider whether, at an appropriate time, further arms control, security and confidence building measures might be addressed, by the competent bodies, taking into account existing obligations and commitments under the CFE Treaty.

(iii) receive regular information from the competent bodies addressing cooperation on defence/military issues aimed at enhancing stability in the region and among countries in the region, and facilitate the sustained engagement of all concerned to ensure regional security, conflict prevention and management. The work of this Table will complement and be coherent with efforts for the security of this region undertaken by various European and Euro-Atlantic initiatives and structures.

D. The Working Tables will establish work plans in conformity with the objectives of the Stability Pact. Within the range of their competence, they can establish side tables or call meetings and conferences on matters of a specific or sub-regional nature. In this context, special attention is to be given to fostering the exchange between private citizens (in particular youth), societal groups, entrepreneurs and companies as well as non-governmental organisations and their respective counterparts in the various countries of the region. They will, in particular, pay attention to the coherence and consistency of their work with existing activities and seek to promote complementarity and synergy, as well as avoid duplication, with existing activities.

E. The Chairmanship of the Working Tables will be established by the South Eastern Europe Regional Table. The Working Tables will report to the South Eastern Europe Regional Table. The respective chairs of the South Eastern Europe Regional Table and the Working Tables will meet periodically and as necessary to discuss and coordinate the activities of the Working Tables and to monitor progress.

F. The location and timing of the individual Working Tables should be arranged to facilitate, to the extent possible, the attendance of participants who may take part in more than one Working Table, without excluding different Tables developing their own calendars according to their respective dynamics. Tables could take place either in rotation in the countries of the region or at the invitation of individual countries or of the European Union or in Vienna, at the venue of the Permanent Council of the OSCE.

G. The host country, or host organisation, should provide at its expense meeting facilities, such as conference rooms, secretarial assistance and interpretation. The European Union has expressed its readiness to bear such expenses when meetings are held at the seat of its institutions.

Index

Abkhazia 105–6
aid programmes 31, 141–2
Albania 103
   aid programmes 31
   decentralisation 31
   democratisation 31, 32–3, 35
   elections 31
   environmental issues 33
   impact of Kosovo crisis 31, 33, 103–4
   media 33
   OSCE Mission xvi, xxi, 30
   political mediation in 32
   role of women in 32
   status report 30–36
Anderson, Norman 49
Annan, Kofi 7
Armenia 106, 107
arms embargoes 70–71
Austria, Yugoslav conflict and 87
Azerbaijan 106, 107

Badinter Report 87
Barra, Jean 73
Barry, Robert xv, xviii, 24, 66, 67
Belarus 107
Bildt, Carl 89
Booth, Ken 73
Bosnia and Herzegovina 103
   democratisation 28–9
   elections xx, 20–21, 22, 26–7, 75, 89
   human rights issues xvii, 27–8
   media xvii, 21
   military forces 21, 24, 98
   ongoing problems 88–9
   OSCE Mission xvi, xx, 24–9
   police 98
   property legislation 21
   refugees returning to 21–2
   role of women in 22
   status report 20–23
Braudel, Fernand 69
broadcast media *see* media

Central European Initiative 141
Charter of Paris 116
Chechnya 107
children's rights issues 108, 120–21
China 73
Cold War 70
Cologne Declaration 56, 104
Contact Group 70, 72, 73, 87
Contact Point 60
Conventional Armed Forces in Europe (CFE) Treaty 86, 110–11, 121–2
corruption 63, 98, 110, 123
Council of Europe xvii, 73, 96–7
   Croatia and 12, 14, 17
   Stability Pact for South-Eastern Europe and 138
Court of Conciliation and Arbitration 127
crime 63, 98, 110, 115
Crimea 108
Croatia 103
   constitutional issues 11–12
   democratisation 14
   discrimination in 13–14
   elections xix–xx, 11, 14, 17–19, 22; Eastern Slavonia 7–8

Croatia (cont'd)
  ethnic violence in 13
  media 15–16
  OSCE Mission xvi, xix–xx, 11,
    12–16
  police xvii, 15; Eastern Slavonia
    8, 10, 103
  property legislation 13
  refugees returning to 13–14
  secession from Yugoslavia 3, 87
  status report 11–19
  United Nations Transitional
    Authority for Eastern
    Slavonia (UNTAES) 3, 4–10,
    15; creation 4–5;
    demilitarisation by 6;
    mandate 5–6; success of 6–9
  war crimes prosecutions 15

Danube Commission 63
Dayton Agreement xvi, 20, 21, 24,
  25, 26, 27, 64, 73, 88
decentralisation
  Albania 31
  Macedonia (Former Yugoslav
    Republic) 44
democratisation xvii, 96
  Albania 31, 32–3, 35
  Bosnia and Herzegovina 28–9
  Croatia 14
  Stability Pact for South-Eastern
    Europe and 47
  Yugoslavia 102
  see also elections
disaster relief 98, 110

economic issues 88, 97, 115
  Istanbul Charter and 122–3
  Macedonia (Former Yugoslav
    Republic) 44
  Stability Pact for South–Eastern
    Europe 57, 62–3
education, Stability Pact for South-
  Eastern Europe and 61–2

elections xvii
  Albania 31
  Bosnia and Herzegovina xx,
    20–21, 22, 26–7, 75, 89
  Croatia xix–xx, 11, 14, 17–19,
    22; Eastern Slavonia 7–8
  Istanbul Charter and 121
  Kosovo xiv, xx, 89
  Macedonia (Former Yugoslav
    Republic) 43–4
Eliasson, Jan 63
environmental issues 108–9
  Albania 33
  Istanbul Charter and 122–3
Erdut Accord (1995) 4
ethnic minorities 109
  Croatia 13
  Gypsies (Roma/Sinti) 46, 59–60,
    97, 109, 120
  Istanbul Charter and 79, 119
  Macedonia (Former Yugoslav
    Republic) 43, 44, 48, 49, 50
  see also refugees
European Bank for Reconstruction
  and Development (EBRD)
  62, 140
European Investment Bank (EIB) 62,
  140
European Union xviii
  Albania and 31
  Istanbul Charter and 81
  Monitoring Mission (ECMM)
    13, 41
  OSCE and xii, xvi, xviii, 65
  recognition of Slovenia and
    Croatia 3
  Stability Pact for South-Eastern
    Europe and 55, 62, 65, 104,
    136–7
  Yugoslav conflict and 71, 74–5

France, Yugoslav conflict and 87
Friends of Albania xxi, 31, 103

Galbraith, Peter W. 4
gender issues *see* women
Georgia 105–6
Germany
   Stability Pact for South-Eastern Europe and 55
   Yugoslav conflict and 87
Gligorov, President 47, 49, 50
Gypsies (Roma/Sinti) 46, 59–60, 97, 109, 120

Hajdari, Azem 32
Helsinki Final Act 116
Hobsbawm, Eric 69
Hombach, Bodo 58
Hoxha, Enver 34
human rights issues xvii, 96–7
   Bosnia and Herzegovina xvii, 27–8
   Croatia 13–14
   Istanbul Charter and 119–21
   Stability Pact for South-Eastern Europe 59–60
   see also ethnic minorities; property legislation; refugees

international aid programmes 31, 141–2
international cooperation xii, xvi, xviii, 69–76, 83–4, 123–4, 136–40, 141
International Monetary Fund 140
Istanbul Charter for European Security (1999) 77–85, 91, 92, 101
   ethnic minorities and 79, 119
   human rights issues 119–21
   institutional issues 79–80, 119
   interface with other security organisations 83–4, 117–18, 127–8, 130–1
   operational capacities for conflict prevention and crisis management 81–3; joint co-operative actions 83; long-term missions 82–3; peacekeeping operations 81–2, 127
   Platform for Co-operative Security 117, 118, 129
   politico-military issues 77–9, 121–2
   security issues 78–9
   text 113–31
Istanbul Summit Declaration 67, 91, 101–12

Jelavic, President 20

Kosovo
   continuing violence in 38, 90
   elections xiv, xx, 89
   European Union and xii
   impact of crisis: on Albania 31, 33, 103–4; on Macedonia 44–5, 50–51, 103–4
   international governmental structure 37–8
   media in xvii, xx
   OSCE mission xiii–xiv, xvi, xx, 85, 101–2
   police xvii, xx, 38
   refugees from 31, 33, 44, 101, 102
   status report 37–8
   United Nations Mission (UNMIK) xii, xvi, 37, 38

local government
   Macedonia (Former Yugoslav Republic) 44, 45
   Stability Pact for South-Eastern Europe and 60

Macedonia (Former Yugoslav Republic) 73, 90, 103
   border monitoring 42–3, 44, 47–8

Macedonia (cont'd)
  decentralisation 44
  economic issues 44
  elections 43–4
  impact of Kosovo crisis on 44–5, 50–51, 103–4
  inter-ethnic relations 43, 44, 48, 49, 50
  local government 44, 45
  OSCE Mission xxi, 41–6, 47–51; activities 42, 47–8; dependence on Macedonian authorities 49–50; mandate 48–9
  police 49
  status report 41–6
map drawing 70
media xvii, 108
  Albania 33
  Bosnia and Herzegovina xvii, 21
  Croatia 15–16
  Istanbul Charter and 121
  Kosovo xvii, xx
  Stability Pact for South-Eastern Europe and 60, 97
Milanovic, Milan 4
military forces 98, 121–2
  Bosnia and Herzegovina 21, 24
  Conventional Armed Forces in Europe (CFE) Treaty 86, 110–11, 121–2
  Stability Pact for South-Eastern Europe and 57
mines 111–12
Moldova 106
Montenegro xx, 90

Nagorno-Karabakh 106
New York Declaration 20
North Atlantic Treaty Organisation (NATO) xii, xviii, 55, 70, 72, 73, 75, 139

Open Skies Treaty 111

Organisation of the Black Sea Economic Cooperation 141
Organisation for Economic Cooperation and Development 140
Organisation for Security and Cooperation in Europe (OSCE)
  advantages of xii
  co-operation with other organisations xii, xvi, xviii, 83–4, 123–4
  creation 91
  institutions 79–80
  missions xvi–xviii, 82–3, 98–9, 124–5; see also individual countries
  Office for Democratic Institutions and Human Rights (ODIHR) 7, 18, 28, 43–4, 45–6, 108
  operational role xii–xiii
  OSCE first principle xi
  peacekeeping operations 81–2, 127
  report on development of south-eastern Europe dimension 95–100; key regional issues 96–8; recommendations 98–100
  see also Istanbul Charter for European Security (1999); Stability Pact for South-Eastern Europe
Owen, David 72

Pavlevic, Vlatko 12
peacekeeping operations 81–2, 127
Petrltsch, Wolfgang xx, 20, 24
Platform for Co–operative Security 117, 118, 129
police xvii–xviii, 126
  Bosnia and Herzegovina 98

police (cont'd)
  Croatia xvii, 15; Eastern
    Slavonia 8, 10, 103
  Kosovo xvii, xx, 38
  Macedonia (Former Yugoslav
    Republic) 49
Poplasen, Nikola 20
press *see* media
preventive diplomacy 86–7
property legislation
  Bosnia and Herzegovina 21
  Croatia 13

Rapid Expert Assistance and
  Cooperation Teams (REACT)
  xi, xvi, 82, 110, 125
refugees 96
  from Kosovo 31, 33, 44, 101,
    102
  returning to Bosnia and
    Herzegovina 21–2
  returning to Croatia 13–14
  Stability Pact for South-Eastern
    Europe and 61
Roma (Gypsies) 46, 59–60, 97, 109,
  120
Royaumont Process 62, 140–41
Russia
  Chechnya and 107
  Istanbul Charter and 77, 78,
    79–80, 83
  Moldova and 106
  Stability Pact for South-Eastern
    Europe and 139–40

Saccomanni, Fabrizio 62
Sarinic, Hrvoje 4
Schoups, Major General 6
security issues 98, 111
  Istanbul Charter and 78–9, 115,
    116, 118, 121–2
  Stability Pact for South–Eastern
    Europe and 64

Sinti/Roma (Gypsies) 46, 59–60, 97,
  109, 120
Skrunda Radar Station 107
Slovenia, secession from Yugoslavia
  3, 87
South East Europe Cooperation
  Initiative (SECI) 62, 141
South Ossetia 105
Stability Pact for South-Eastern
  Europe xiv–xv, xvi, xviii, xix,
    34, 51, 55–68, 73, 89, 95,
    104, 118
  actors 56–7, 132–3; co-operation
    between 136–40
  annex 142–4
  democratisation and 47
  economic issues 57, 62–3
  education and 61–2
  human rights issues 59–60
  implementation 59–64, 142
  local government and 60
  mechanisms 135–6
  media and 60, 97
  military forces and 57
  objectives 57–8, 134–5
  OSCE's relation to xiv, xv, xix,
    55, 64–7, 99–100, 104, 137–8
  principles and norms 133
  refugees and 61
  role of women and 60–61, 96
  security issues 64
  structures of 58
  text 132–44
Stockholm Convention (1992) 127
Stoel, Max van der 43, 112
Stoltenberg, Thorvald 4, 72

terrorism 115
Tito, Marshall 34
Tokmadzija, Drago 88–9
Tudjman, Franjo 11, 19
Turkey 110

Ukraine 107–8
United Kingdom
    Stability Pact for South-Eastern
        Europe and 63
    Yugoslav conflict and 87
United Nations xvii, 116, 117
    High Commissioner for Refugees
        (UNHCR) 13, 14, 61, 138
    Kosovo Mission (UNMIK) xii,
        xvi, 37, 38
    OSCE and xii
    Protection Force (UNPROFOR)
        in Yugoslavia 3
    Stability Pact for South-Eastern
        Europe and 138, 139
    Transitional Authority for
        Eastern Slavonia (UNTAES)
        3, 4–10, 15; creation 4–5;
        demilitarisation by 6;
        mandate 5–6; success of 6–9
    Yugoslav conflict and 71–2, 87
United States of America
    Istanbul Charter and 81
    recognition of Slovenia and
        Croatia 3
    Stability Pact for South-Eastern
        Europe and 63
    Yugoslav conflict and 70–71, 73,
        75

van der Stoel, Max 43, 112
Vance, Cyrus 48
Vranitzky, Franz 30

war crimes prosecutions, Croatia 15
Western European Union (WEU) 71,
    140
Woltmann, Dieter 20
women 109
    in Albania 32
    in Bosnia and Herzegovina 22
    Istanbul Charter and 120–21
    Stability Pact for South-Eastern
        Europe and 60–61, 96
World Bank 62, 140, 141–2
World Trade Organisation (WTO)
    63

Yugoslavia, Federal Republic of
    xx–xxi, 55, 102
    break-up of 3, 87
    democratisation 102
    Stability Pact for South-Eastern
        Europe and 56
    United Nations Protection Force
        (UNPROFOR) 3